Perspectives in Health Humanities

UC Health Humanities Press publishes scholarship produced or reviewed under the auspices of the University of California Health Humanities Consortium, a multi-campus collaborative of faculty, students, and trainees in the humanities, medicine, and health sciences. Our series invites scholars from the humanities and healthcare professions to share narratives and analysis on health, healing, and the contexts of our beliefs and practices that impact biomedical inquiry.

General Editor

Brian Dolan, PhD, Professor, Department of Humanities and Social Sciences, University of California, San Francisco (UCSF)

Other Titles in this Series

Heart Murmurs: What Patients Teach Their Doctors
Edited by Sharon Dobie, MD (2014)

Humanitas: Readings in the Development of the Medical Humanities
Edited by Brian Dolan (2015)

Follow the Money: Funding Research in a Large Academic Health Center
Henry R. Bourne and Eric B. Vermillion (2016)

Soul Stories: Voices from the Margins
Josephine Ensign (2018)

Fixing Women: The Birth of Obstetrics and Gynecology in Britain and America
Marcia D. Nichols (2021)

Autobiography of a Sea Creature: Healing the Trauma of Infant Surgery
Wendy P. Williams (2023)

Medical Humanities, Cultural Humility, and Social Justice
Edited by Dalia Magaña, Christina Lux, and Ignacio López-Calvo (2023)

I0039954

www.UCHealthHumanitiesPress.com

This series is made possible by the generous support of the Dean of the School of Medicine at UCSF, the UCSF Library, and a Multicampus Research Program Grant from the University of California Office of the President. Grant ID MR-15-328363 and Grant ID M23PR5992.

Why Is U.S. Healthcare So Costly

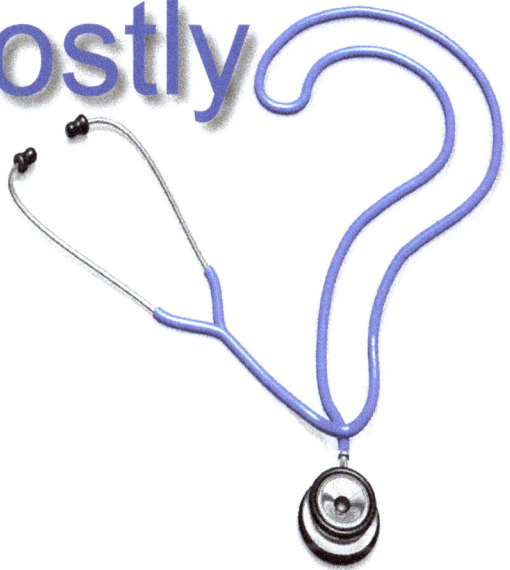

A Brief History of (Not) Controlling Healthcare Costs in America

Brian Dolan, PhD &
Stephen Beitler, PhD

University of California
Center for Health Humanities
Department of Humanities and Social Sciences
UCSF (Box 0850)
490 Illinois Street, Floor 7
San Francisco, CA 94143-0850

Designed by Virtuoso Press

Library of Congress Control Number: 2024949143

ISBN (print): 979-8-9899229-5-6

Printed in USA

Contents

Preface

This book began as a graduate seminar at the University of California-San Francisco titled "The Making of American Healthcare." That seminar explored how different medical industry sectors have contributed to ever-rising healthcare costs. It also made clear how healthcare participants, including patients, have steadily denied their own responsibilities for costs. Our first title for the book was "Healthcare Costs in America: 100 Years of Finger-Pointing."

We thought an historical lens could help people see how professional, governmental, and commercial sectors, each acting in their own interests, had contributed to this outcome; and how efforts to control costs have failed consistently.

Our goal was to help readers understand, as we have tried to, what the past can teach us about prices we pay for healthcare today. How did we get to this point?

We knew we couldn't tell the whole story, so we decided to write a *primer* on healthcare costs. A terrific model was *Smart Brevity*, a book by writers at the Axios media network. They showed how to address complex topics concisely. We challenged ourselves to craft a compelling narrative in a format that bears little resemblance to standard historical texts. We will leave it to readers to assess how well we did.

There are other things that this book is not. Even though we have relied extensively on the work of healthcare economists, this is *not* an economics book. It's also not a polemic. There are many studies of healthcare that start from a preference either for market-based or government-led approaches. We're happy to leave that debate to the policy and politics communities.

Instead, this is a small sliver of the epic story of healthcare costs in America. We're trained as historians of medicine, and we relish the privilege of studying a complex past through an historical lens. Of course, we're responsible for any factual errors.

So if the big picture shows medical-industry sectors pursuing their own interests and pointing fingers on costs, does the historical record suggest any unifying themes?

Here's our list:

Information asymmetry – Even with Google, patients' interactions with doctors are defined by large gaps in medical knowledge. That's why people go to doctors. This imbalance, and the resulting power differential, is a starting point for high costs.

Physician autonomy – American clinicians have consistently achieved decisive control of how they *practice* medicine, largely self-monitored and free of government influence. By contrast, healthcare *funding* has a lot to do with government.

Insurance-based payers – The role of commercial insurance in healthcare started about 100 years ago and has grown steadily. It has been a building block of a broad financialization of American healthcare.

Disease, condition, and prevention marketing – Scholars and journalists have shown how pharmaceutical and device companies, professional groups, and media outlets help energize beliefs in medical need, deficiency, and threat among Americans.

Technology imperatives – It's an axiom of healthcare narratives that Americans want, and expect, the latest advances applied to their health.

Legislative support – Over the last century, the US Congress has enacted numerous laws that have shaped how healthcare works and how it gets paid for.

Regulatory passivity – America's Food and Drug Administration (FDA), the nation's gatekeeper for medical treatments and devices, traditionally has been underfunded, understaffed, and increasingly financed by pharmaceutical companies.

We believe that America's distinctively high healthcare costs result from an economic mismatch and decisive knowledge control. A key historical question – Who decides? – runs through the story.

So let's start at the top.

How About a Top-Ten Recommended Reading List to Get Things Started?

This is a small sampling of the vast body of scholarship and journalism that examines American healthcare from many perspectives.

1. John Abramson. *Sickening: How Big Pharma Broke American Health Care – and How We Can Repair It.* Boston: Mariner Books, 2022.
2. David Dranove and Lawton R. Burns. *Big Med: Megaproviders and the High Cost of Health Care in America.* Chicago: The University of Chicago Press, 2021.
3. Joseph Dumit. *Drugs for Life: How Pharmaceutical Companies Define Our Health.* Durham: Duke University Press, 2012.
4. Liran Einav and Amy Finkelstein. *We've Got You Covered: Rebooting American Health Care.* New York: Portfolio/Penguin, 2023.
5. Ben Goldacre. *Bad Pharma: How Drug Companies Mislead Doctors and Harm Patients.* New York: Faber and Faber, Inc., 2012.
6. Vivian S. Lee. *The Long Fix: Solving America's Health Care Crisis with Strategies That Work for Everyone.* New York: W. W. Norton & Company, 2020.
7. Marty Makary. *The Price We Pay: What Broke American Health Care – and How to Fix It.* New York: Bloomsbury Publishing, 2021.
8. James C. Robinson. *The Corporate Practice of Medicine: Competition and Innovation in Health Care.* Berkeley: University of California Press, 1999.
9. Elisabeth Rosenthal. *An American Sickness: How Healthcare Became Big Business and How You Can Take It Back.* New York: Penguin Books, 2017.
10. Ilana Yurkiewicz. *Fragmented: A Doctor's Quest to Piece Together American Health Care.* New York: W. W. Norton & Company, 2023.

Overview

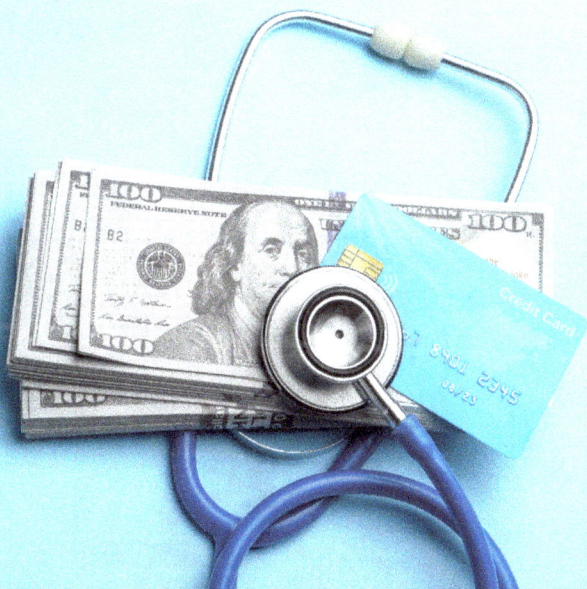

There is no shortage of scholarship documenting continuously increasing healthcare costs in America. Nor is there a lack of theories as to why costs keep rising.

Why It Matters

Our approach differs from most other discussions of healthcare. We did not want to start from a stance of advocating either market competition or the role of the federal government as a guiding principle of our study. We feel that focusing on key players and the historical record could help people see how prices have kept going up.

This chapter introduces themes that connect the diverse forces affecting healthcare costs.

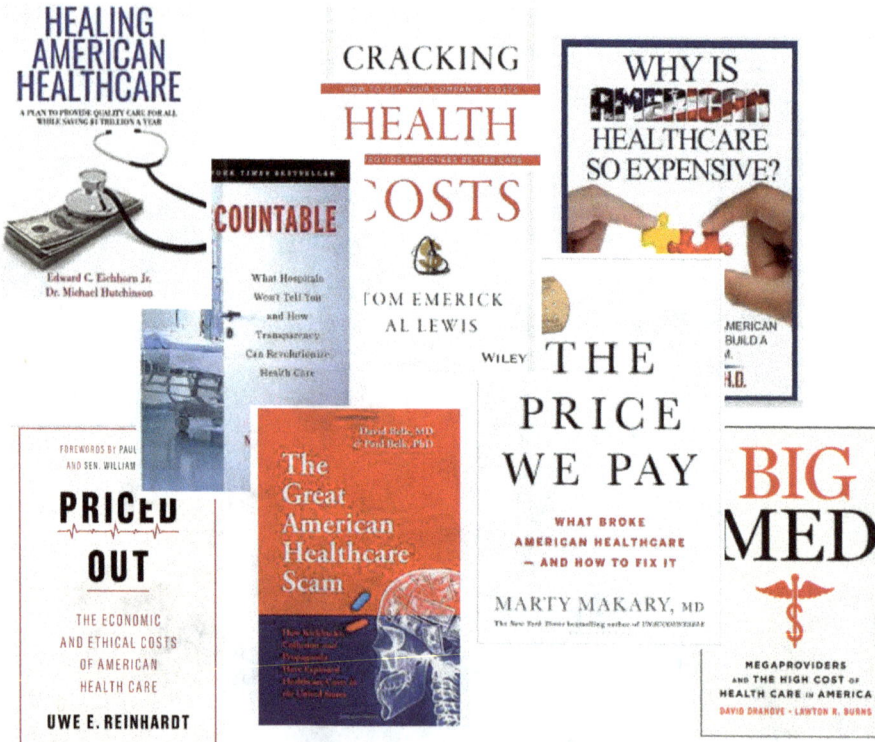

The U.S. is a world outlier when it comes to health care spending.

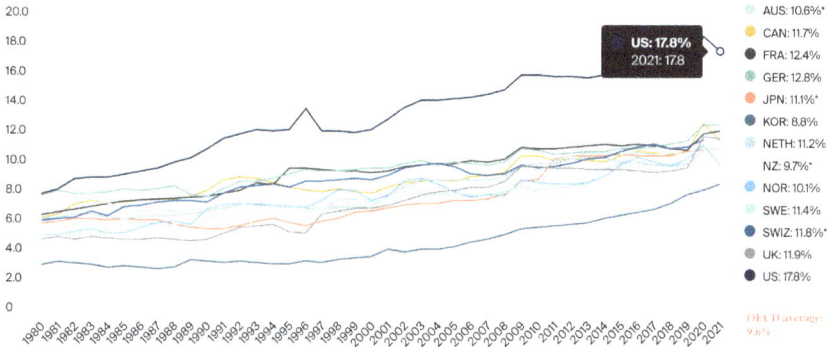

Percent of GDP spent on health, 1980–2021*

US: 17.8%
2021: 17.8

2021 data (or latest available year)*:

AUS: 10.6%*
CAN: 11.7%
FRA: 12.4%
GER: 12.8%
JPN: 11.1%*
KOR: 8.8%
NETH: 11.2%
NZ: 9.7%*
NOR: 10.1%
SWE: 11.4%
SWIZ: 11.8%*
UK: 11.9%
US: 17.8%

OECD average: 9.6%

(From Gunja et al. 2023)

By The Numbers

Any way one looks at it, US healthcare is unusually costly.

As total expenditure or percent of gross domestic product (GDP):

In 1970, US healthcare spending was near $75 billion, or $356 per resident, or 7.2 percent of GDP.

In 2007, US healthcare spending was near $2.2 trillion, or $7,500 per resident, or 16.2 percent of GDP.

In 2021, US healthcare spending was near $4.3 trillion, or $12,914 per resident, or 18.3 percent of GDP.

(Sources: Organization for Economic Cooperation and Development 2009; Center for Medicare and Medicaid Services, NHE Factsheet 2023)

Total and Per Capita Spending on Health Care, 1965 to 2005

(Per capita in thousands of 2005 dollars)   (Total in trillions of 2005 dollars)

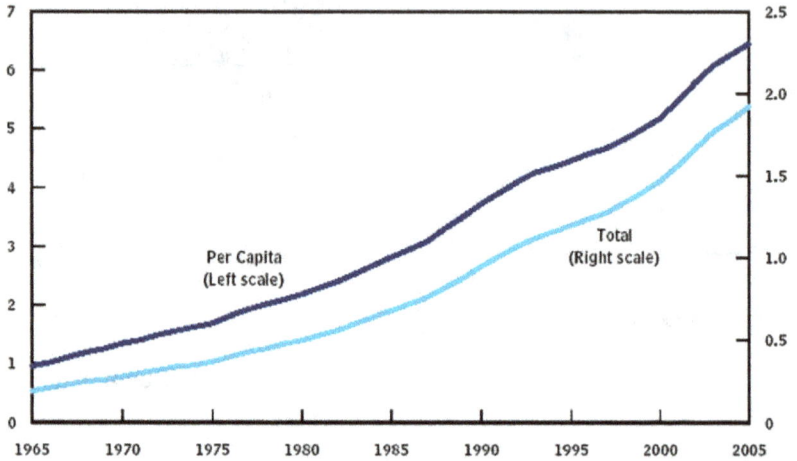

Source: Congressional Budget Office based on data on spending on health services and supplies, as defined in the national health expenditure accounts, maintained by the Centers for Medicare and Medicaid Services.

Long-term projections are fraught with weaknesses and are anything but historical documents. Still, here's what the Congressional Budget Office anticipates:

Projected Spending on Health Care as a Percentage of Gross Domestic Product, 2007 to 2082

(Percent)

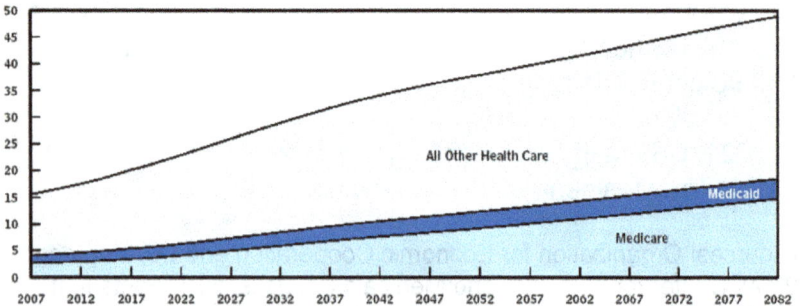

Source: Congressional Budget Office.

Note: Amounts for Medicare are net of beneficiaries' premiums. Amounts for Medicaid are federal spending only.

Economists expect continued growth in healthcare costs for everything: out-of-pocket spending, hospital stays, physician and clinical services, prescription drugs, government programs, and employer premiums.

Those same economists worry when the **rate of growth in costs over time** exceeds the rate of GDP (Gross Domestic Product) growth. This makes healthcare costs a higher proportion of people's *total* expenses.

Every participant in healthcare has contributed to higher costs and has a role in trying to control them.

What is clear in what follows is that costs generated by any participant create opportunities and pressure for others to raise their costs *and to point to others* as the culprits. Many bucks have been passed, literally and otherwise, among healthcare players in the last 100 years.

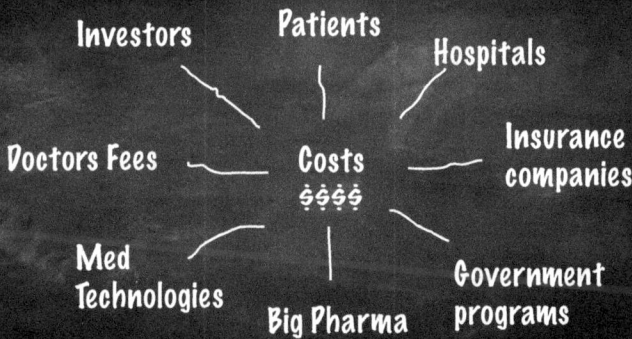

Cost Means Different Things to Different People

Why It Matters

While there has been widespread agreement among Americans that healthcare is expensive, costs are not experienced or perceived the same way by everyone.

Money that flows through the healthcare system is accounted for in different ways, making it difficult to identify culprits of inflated budgets.

As Arora and colleagues (2015) explain, terms such as cost, price, charge, copayment, and reimbursement have different meanings in different contexts depending on who is using the term.

☞ Across the healthcare system, costs will vary depending on insurance coverage, rate negotiations between payers and providers, government regulations, and the interpretation of billing codes.

Defining Terms

Cost refers to the total expenditure involved in the provision of healthcare (wages, supplies, capital expenses, prescriptions, etc.)

Price is the amount that is billed for healthcare, and can vary depending on who is getting billed and who is doing the billing. For an insurer, it is the amount they are responsible for covering.

Copay is the amount a patient is obligated to pay their insurers as part of their access to healthcare.

Charge is the typical rate set by a healthcare provider for a particular service or product.

Reimbursement is the amount of money that a healthcare provider receives from an insurer for services rendered to patients.

"Costly" Refers to Overall Expense, But *Costs* Are Incurred In Different Ways

Patients have costs, whether a copay, an insurance premium, or the whole medical bill.

Providers incur operating costs to produce goods and services.

Hospitals incur costs in capital investment, maintenance, and technology.

Insurers incur costs when their clients utilize healthcare services and products.

Drug companies incur costs for R&D, clinical trials, and marketing.

Governments (whether federal or state) incur costs for healthcare programs and combatting fraud.

A History of Finger Pointing

Everyone wants their costs to go down, but each participant in the healthcare system thinks the problem lies elsewhere.

Patients think it's doctors' salaries and the cost of malpractice insurance and lawsuits.

Doctors say hospital corporations are squeezing the system for profits and that the government is not reimbursing enough for Medicare and Medicaid patients.

Hospitals say that the costs of labor are skyrocketing and technologies that doctors and patients want to use are expensive.

Insurers say that manufacturers' prices for drugs are too high and that doctors overtreat.

Drug companies say that government regulations make drug development costly.

Government agencies point to our aging population and insurance industry practices that require employers and patients to bear more of the risks of coverage.

It's Expensive, But Aims to Be Profitable

Why It Matters

No one participant in the healthcare sector will voluntarily take less money; to control costs, every component of healthcare has to be managed across diverse systems.

The United States is unique, especially among other high-income countries, in the degree to which profit motives and private entities play a role in healthcare delivery.

As one anonymous reviewer of this book put it, America doesn't really have a healthcare system. With private insurance, it's basically free-market. Medicare and Medicaid are largely single-payer. For veterans, we have a smaller-scale version of a nationalized healthcare system.

It's The Market That Drives Up Healthcare Costs

The economic model that dominates American thinking about healthcare reflects a conventional producer-consumer dynamic in which consumer choice in goods and services is crucial.

Medical advertising seeks to capitalize on this, convincing consumers that any cost-control measures are tantamount to controlling freedom of choice. (Tomes 2001)

History shows great reluctance by Washington to intervene in large swaths of the medical marketplace or to encroach the American faith in the marketplace.

Why Is Cost Control So Difficult to Analyze?

Costs Are Part of a Web of Interactions

Just as there is no healthcare "system," there is no single healthcare market. Despite the recent trend of healthcare consolidation into what authors David Dranove and Lawton R. Burns call "megaproviders" (2021), the industry is fed by sub-sectors ranging from AI therapeutics to administrative workflow technologies.

In practice, the organization and delivery of healthcare are an assemblage of smaller component parts that compete for a piece of the $4.3 trillion healthcare pie (patients' needs, industry wages, drugs, technologies, etc.).

Assessing costs and trying to rationalize them based on the activity of the consumer market defies the unique dynamic among consumers (patients), providers (healthcare labor force), and producers (of drugs and biotechnologies), and – most uniquely – the presence of third-party payers (insurers or government programs).

VISIBLE COSTS

HIDDEN COSTS

The Irony of Cost Invisibility

The rapid growth of health insurance plans and government financed healthcare has made healthcare costs the burden of insurers responsible for reimbursement and not hospitals or the medical staff. In fact, because of the way third-party payments have been administered, physicians and patients have been less aware of the cost of medical services at time of delivery. The irony is that families anticipate high healthcare costs because of advanced treatments, but few understand how such costs are calculated or what they will be.

> *"Americans have gotten more tests, seen more physicians, spent more time in hospitals for minor medical procedures, taken more drugs, had more medical examinations, and been subjected to more unnecessary surgery than any other people in the world. **And it has all seemed free.**"* (Califano 1986, p. 56)

> *"The peculiarity was that many patients did not have to pay much for the commodity they consumed. Indeed, **they did not relate to healthcare as a commodity at all,** nor did they consider 'consuming' it as a market transaction. For the secure working class, healthcare stood outside the economy, in a decommodified zone whose logic more closely resembled the family than the market."* (Winant 2021, p. 158)

In Summary

☞ While it easy to agree that US healthcare costs are problematically high, it is difficult to reach consensus about what steps should be taken to control escalating costs.

☞ The healthcare economy defies conventional logic about competition bringing down costs, despite the fact that American consumers (patients) prefer to see healthcare as a product that the are at liberty to shop around for, rather than a public service or nationalized administration of essential care.

☞ Advances in healthcare – servicing a growing, aging, population with new technologies and drugs – certainly come at a cost. The management of chronic diseases through such advances results in long-term cost growth, puting healthcare out of reach for unin-sured or under-insured individuals. The result: the US ranks lowe than other developed countries on various indicators, such as life expectancy, infant mortality rates, and rates of chronic disease.

So what makes it all so expensive, and why can't these costs be contained?

The following chapters look at different healthcare sectors with these questions in mind.

1

Patients

Americans perceive healthcare to be exceedingly expensive, but have historically resisted government intervention or managed care in favor of market-based healthcare.

Why It Matters

It's a healthcare conundrum. Throughout the last century, public opinion polls show that Americans feel that federal assistance to pay medical bills should be offered to poorer and elderly citizens, providing equitable and affordable essential healthcare. However, the public also doesn't trust the government to manage decisions and does not want interference in market-based services—the very thing that most people believe creates barriers to accessing healthcare.

How Cost Concerns Have Trended

A study of twenty-five years of public opinion regarding **why healthcare is so costly** by Blendon, et al. (2006) found that:

- A majority of Americans believed that hospital charges (62%) and the price of prescription drugs (58%) were unreasonably high
- 35% of Americans (in 2005) attributed rising healthcare costs to the profits made by drug and insurance companies
- 19% cited the high number of malpractice lawsuits
- 14% named the greed and waste in the healthcare system
- 8% held the costs of medical technology and drugs to be responsible

Why Are People Disgruntled With Healthcare? (Hint: Costs Keep Rising)

"I didn't know that hospitals and doctors care more about getting paid and where their money is coming from than saving your life. They'll let you sit up there and die if you don't have insurance. And it's just mind-boggling, OK?"

(Patient interviewed in Raudenbush 2020, p. 48)

"Something that always bugs me is that you call and make you an appointment and that's the first thing they want to know is what type of insurance do you have? It's not like, 'Are you afraid you're dying of cervical cancer?' It's like, 'Do you have insurance?'"

("Crissy" as quoted in Fletcher 2016, p. 18)

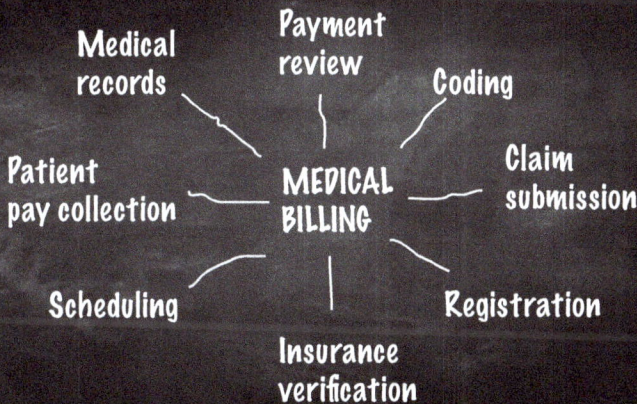

Medical records

Payment review

Coding

Patient pay collection

MEDICAL BILLING

Claim submission

Scheduling

Registration

Insurance verification

Americans Fear Debt More Than Death

Why It Matters

Fearing medical bills leads to bad health outcomes. People forgo medical visits, tests, or treatments because of concern over the high cost of healthcare and out-of-pocket expenses. This exacerbates healthcare disparities between wealthier and well-insured individuals and under- or uninsured and poor individuals.

Affordability Is Considered A National Crisis

Over the last century, Americans have increasingly considered the cost of healthcare among the largest problems facing the nation. A Pew Research Survey in April 2021 found that the affordability of healthcare was identified by **56% of those surveyed as a major problem facing the nation**, holding a 7% lead over the federal deficit and a bigger lead over other issues including violent crime, gun violence, unemployment, and education. (In 2022, this issue dropped to second largest problem after inflation.)

Over the past century, technological advances and specialization in medicine have expanded opportunities for healthcare provision for certain segments of the population, but at a great cost. Patients not only see this as a problem with the healthcare system, but as a problem for managing their own individual health. Why? They want the latest medical advances at their service, but know they may not be able to afford it.

According to Kluender, et al., and data from Kaiser Family Foundation, "Two in five Americans have medical debt, nearly half of whom owe at least $2,500. Due to increasing patient cost-sharing, medical debt is common even among households with health insurance. Among households with medical debt, 63% report reducing expenditures on food and clothing and 48% report using up all or most of their savings because of medical debt." (Kluender et al. 2024)

A majority of Americans say the affordability of health care is a very big problem in the country today

% who say each of the following is ____ in the country today

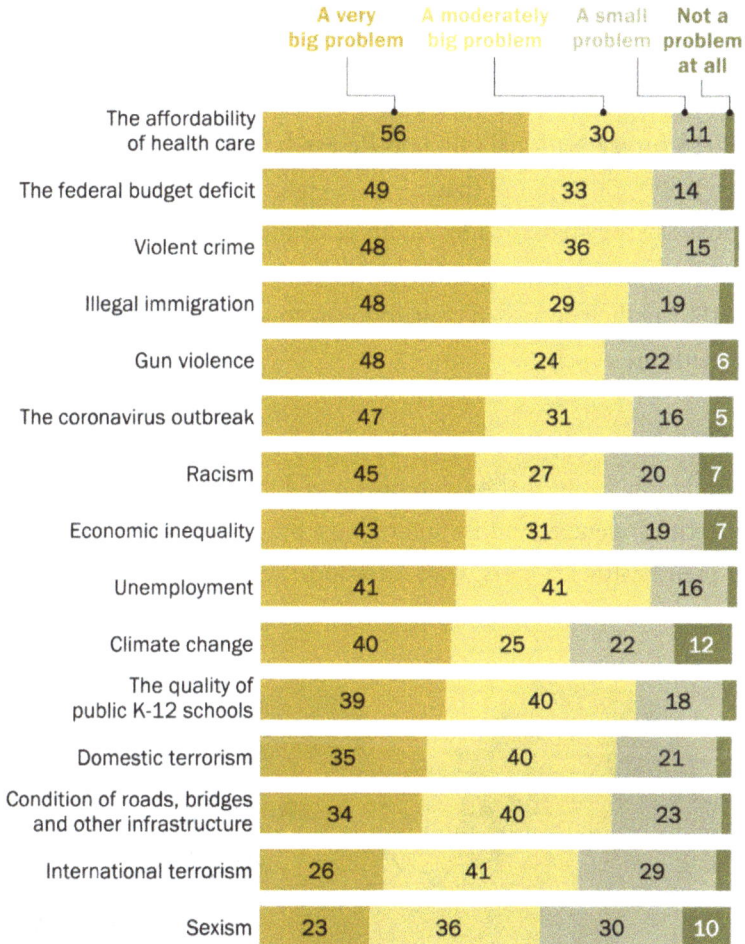

	A very big problem	A moderately big problem	A small problem	Not a problem at all
The affordability of health care	56	30	11	
The federal budget deficit	49	33	14	
Violent crime	48	36	15	
Illegal immigration	48	29	19	
Gun violence	48	24	22	6
The coronavirus outbreak	47	31	16	5
Racism	45	27	20	7
Economic inequality	43	31	19	7
Unemployment	41	41	16	
Climate change	40	25	22	12
The quality of public K-12 schools	39	40	18	
Domestic terrorism	35	40	21	
Condition of roads, bridges and other infrastructure	34	40	23	
International terrorism	26	41	29	
Sexism	23	36	30	10

Survey of US adults conducted April 5-11, 2021. Pew Research Center.

A 2016 study found that 43% of low-income adults ages 19–64 in the United States reported being **unable to access healthcare because of the associated costs,** such as going to the doctor or getting a prescription filled. (Osborn et al. 2016)

By The Numbers

Studies published in 2014 and 2015 estimated that **30% of Americans have difficulty paying medical bills**. (Richman and Brodie 2014; Collins et al. 2015)

A 2018 survey National Opinion Research Center (NORC 2018) of over 1,300 adults found that:
- 36% say they have had to use up all or most of their savings
- 32% report borrowing money or increasing credit card debt
- 41% say they decreased contributions to a savings plan because of healthcare expenses

A 2022 survey (Lopes et al. 2022) of over 2,300 adults by Kaiser Family Foundation found that **41% report owed medical debt** to credit cards, collections agencies, family and friends, banks, and other lenders to pay for their healthcare costs, with disproportionate shares of Black and Hispanic adults carrying healthcare debt.

Concern Over Healthcare Costs Depends On Who Is Paying

The costliness of healthcare is associated with specific financial trans-actions, some of which are invisible to consumers. For those seeking healthcare, the cost concern is what they have to pay. If it's their insurers or the government, costliness is less a concern.

A Pew Research Center survey in 2006 found that approximately **60-65% of Americans perceive a negative impact on American families resulting from costs of insurance premiums**, copays, deduct-ibles, and direct costs of services, products, and prescription medicines. (Blendon et al. 2006)

Insurance Offers No Assurance of Debt-Free Medical Care

Rarely does insurance cover all medical costs. Research by Kaiser Family Foundation (Pollitz et al. 2014) found that

70% of Americans with medical debt had health insurance

Over the last century, patients have seen the construction of a system predicated on insurance coverage as a means of access to healthcare. However, insurance coverage is increasingly expensive for individuals to buy and unreliable as an employment perk.

> *We came here to work but things have not worked out like we thought. After ten years we are still trying. We did not come here for that [Medicaid]. … I think we need some help here … to have medical services like everybody else. We are Hispanic and we don't make much money. We are not like those whites that make six figures and don't need help.*

Julissa, a 54-year-old Dominican who moved to Miami (interviewed between 2012-2013; Calvo et al. 2017)

Immigrants in Florida, a state that sued to avoid expanding coverage under the Affordable Care Act, search for coverage in the private insurance market. However, premium payments and high copayments made having private insurance unaffordable. (Calvo et al. 2017)

It's Understood: Unlimited Demand Drives Up Healthcare Costs

Why It Matters

Americans tolerate income-based healthcare disparities because the market, rather than "socialist" attempts by the government to control healthcare costs, is the American way. (Hero et al. 2017)

> **"** *Americans exhibited less moral concern about income-based differences in the quality of healthcare that people have access to, compared to respondents in the majority of the other countries.*
>
> (Conclusion from Hero et al. 2017)

Bottom Line

Americans see health disparities as a consequence of inequitable access to market-based healthcare, which is open to those with purchasing power but prohibitive for those without.

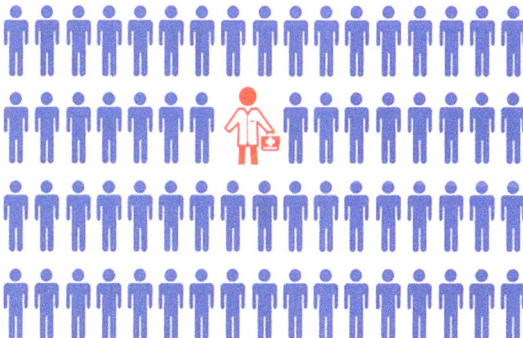

Racism And The Fear Of Socialism Have Hindered Healthcare Reform In America

Two reasons the public have rejected healthcare reform

Despite wanting to pay less for healthcare and seeing rising costs as a national problem, two forces persuade the public to resist reform:

1. A **history of racism** that prevents extending social services to people of color (including Social Security, Fair Labor Standards, and G.I. Bill assistance). (Interlandi 2019)
2. A manipulative political discourse that **national healthcare is socialist and un-American.** (Dolan 2016)

Major National Healthcare Reform Debates

⇾	1940s	Truman administration (fail)
⇾	1961-65	Kennedy/Johnson administration (passed Medicare)
⇾	1971-74	Nixon administration (fail)
⇾	1993-94	Clinton administration (fail)
⇾	2008-10	Obama administration (passed Affordable Care Act)

Why It Matters

Fear-mongering, political machinations, and polarized rhetoric cause people to vote against the majority interest in affordable healthcare.

Throughout the twentieth century, Americans have wanted help paying medical bills. Prior to each of the major federal bills introducing national healthcare insurance, polls showed that between 66-82% of the public **support measures to reduce healthcare costs** to individuals. (Blendon and Benson 2001) But they often fail at the ballot box.

For Poorer, Under- Or Uninsured Individuals, Healthcare Means Self-Care

Where the healthcare "system" fails, the market for alternative and complementary remedies emerges

Communities of color have endured a long history of structural racism in seeking access to mainstream healthcare, being denied entirely or receiving poor quality care. The continued strength of self-care practices is affirmed in an analysis of national survey data among African Americans, in which almost 70% reported that their families used home remedies. (Boyd 2000)

☞ The development of spiritual strength is used to combat the problems of being uninsured

"I just tell the Lord, 'Please, I just hope I don't have no problems because I don't know how in the hell I'm going to pay for it.' It's the mind, it's the mind that heals a lot of things on your body. That's how I deal with it. If I can be strong-minded and not cause my mind to break down and cause it to really bring me down, physically or mentally."

50-year-old unemployed and uninsured man with chronic back pain (Becker et al. 2004, p. 2070)

Keyword: Subsistence Entrepreneur

Viswanathan and colleagues (2014) describe "**subsistence entrepreneurs**" as low-income individuals who live in communities with intense interpersonal relationships and rely exclusively on these social networks to sustain and stabilize their businesses, including the informal market for medical goods.

'Subsistence Entrepreneurs' Create Their Own Medical Marketplace

Low-income communities create social networks that allow them to participate in an underground market in medicines and medical devices to receive care.

There are several different types of medications available off the street, including prescription strength ibuprofen, antibiotics, asthma inhalers, allergy medicine, hypertension medication, insulin, and Vicodin. There are also various kinds of medical equipment, including canes, walkers, and wheelchairs. (Raudenbush 2020, p. 65)

For Immigrants to America, Healthcare Costs Are Unchallengeable and Part of the Perceived Power of American Institutions

Why It Matters

Immigrant populations, regardless of legal status, face unique challenges accessing American healthcare because of language difficulties, cultural differences, barriers to federal support, and lack of insurance in low-paying jobs. (Stone, et al. 2019; Wilson et al. 2020)

Case In Point

"Manuel, a 32-year-old Cuban who earns $700 a week to provide for a family of four, including an infant, told us:

We got insurance for my son but it did not cover everything. Every time we needed to go to the doctor we had to think if we could pay. We had to calculate if we had money for the copayments, the exams and the medication and enough to cover the car insurance, and the rent for the month. We had to drop it at the end." (Calvo et al. 2017)

Historically, Healthcare Wasn't Worth Paying For

The concern over healthcare costs emerged and grew throughout the twentieth century.

A healthcare marketplace that sold the promise of miracle cures helped create income-based disparities. Before the twentieth century, medical practice had very little scientific knowledge to tout and a poor track record of helping patients. Paradoxically, healthcare was the most equal when there was less of it because it couldn't do much for anyone regardless of their income.

☞ **Nineteenth-century America praised the "self-help" philosophy of healthcare.**

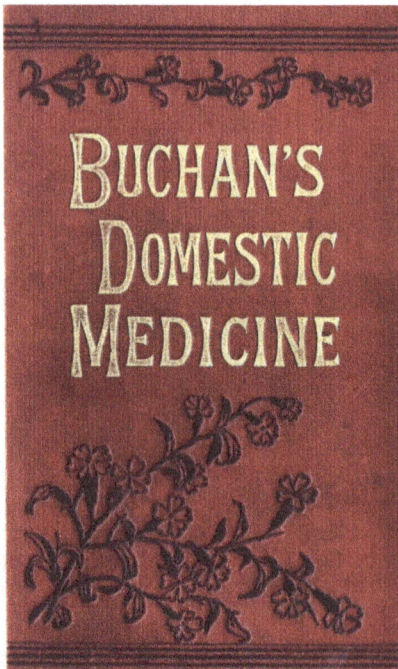

Scottish physician William Buchan published his wildly successful book in 1769, which intended to educate families on self-care through home remedies.

Historical Note on Self-Help

In the 1830s, President Andrew Jackson promoted a political philosophy that championed greater democracy for the "common man" as distinct from aristocratic privileges to govern. Historians refer to this as "Jacksonian democracy." Medical historians have used this reference to frame state resistance to medical licensing laws that were intended to restrict the practice of medicine to doctors with a recognized level of training. The rationale for the rejection of professional qualifications (that were intended to protect the public from quackery) was based on the rejection of elitism in favor of "domestic medicine," the concept of household health management and individualism as a virtue over reliance on privileged authority.

Samuel Thomson, celebrated namesake of the "Thomsonian movement" in nineteenth-century American medicine, advocated for the treatment of disorders using natural remedies. A New Hampshire farmer turned self-educated botanical healer, Thomson believed that families could develop a domestic healing routine – called "kitchen physick" earlier in Europe – that used garden herbs, vegetables, and steam baths to treat common ailments. (Appel 2010)

Thomson was a popular promoter of self-help in America. Eventually, the medical profession's interest in controlling knowledge and therapies led to regulations on practice that created the modern medical profession and its concentration on biochemical investigation and treatment of disease.

American Healthcare Has Been a Business From the Beginning, and Not a Public Good

Americans believe in the moral imperative for healthcare, but historically have committed to a free market provision instead of collective action.

According to Alain Enthoven and Sara Singer of Stanford University, "most people consider it unacceptable for people to suffer, to be disabled, or to have shortened lives because they cannot pay for care. In a sense universal access to necessary healthcare is a public good." (Coombs 2005, p. 267)

☞ **This is the healthcare paradox: it's immoral to allow suffering, but against the economic imperative of self-interest to pay for someone else's care.**

Americans Like to Shop for Drugs

Why It Matters

Americans have been conditioned to see modern medicine as a product of consumer capitalism, where patients are equivalent to shoppers searching for quality, value, and variety. Marketing strategies tout that there's **a pill for every ill,** with the pharmaceutical industry expanding diagnoses to increase demand for their drugs. (Moyniham and Cassels 2005)

Direct-to-consumer marketing of drugs could …

lead patients to pressure physicians to prescribe unnecessary or unindicated drugs, increase the price of drugs, confuse patients by leading them to believe that some minor difference represents a major therapeutic advance, potentiate the use of brand name products rather than cheaper, but equivalent generic drugs and foster increased drug taking."

FDA Commissioner Arthur Hull Hayes in 1983 (Donohue 2006, p. 676)

The Marketing Problem

Treating healthcare as a conventional commodity enables advertisers to encourage unnecessary use of pharmaceutical products. In this model, marketing affects consumer behavior more than medical knowledge.

American consumers of healthcare products want more information to guide their purchasing decisions, and the pharmaceutical industry answered.

Direct-to-consumer marketing totals around $6.5 billion annually (in 2020) in ads for prescription drugs. *Source*: Pharmaceutical Research and Manufacturers of America (PhRMA)

Historical Note on Medical Marketing

In the nineteenth century, ubiquitous advertising and traveling salesmen helped shape Americans' attitudes toward the medical marketplace. Ads were on every broadsheet page, circulated around streets on postcards, and plastered on the side of buildings. (Hilts 2003)

A century-long ad campaign by the healthcare industry convinced the American public that they were sick in varied ways and could shop for miracle cures. As historian Nancy Tomes writes in her book *How Madison Avenue and Modern Medicine Turned Patients Into Consumers*, "**producing sick people was a better business model than keeping them well**." (Tomes 2001, p. 164)

Frustrated with rising costs and uncertainty about the value and risks of what the pharmaceutical industry was selling, in the 1960s and 1970s patient advocacy groups agitated for transparency in information (such as drug ingredients) and truth in advertising. While new regulations (such as FDA-guided package labeling) cleaned up marketing practices, the healthcare industry stressed the importance of "doctor shopping" and exercising freedom of choice for consumers to obtain their preferred healthcare options. (Donohue 2006)

Case in Point: "In 2000 Merck spent more advertising its new painkiller, Vioxx ($160 million) than was spent on advertising for Budweiser ($146 million), Pepsi ($125 million), or Nike ($78 million). That year drug sales for Vioxx topped $1.5 billion and twenty-five million people took the drug. That success proved tragic. Researchers ultimately concluded that the drug caused eighty-eight thousand heart attacks, nearly half of them fatal. In 2004 Merck withdrew Vioxx from the market. The company ultimately paid a criminal fine of $950 million for its marketing and sales tactics." (Rosenthal 2018, p. 100)

→ **Consumer-driven, free-enterprise medicine assumes a knowledgeable consumer, but most patients are not knowledgeable about healthcare or their medical needs.**

Patients Are Ill-Equipped Consumers in the Healthcare Marketplace

- A national survey of nearly 2,000 people in 2020 by Harris Poll showed that 62% believe the healthcare system is designed to be confusing, 61% reported their bills feel more complex than a mortgage payment, and two-thirds said they are asked to manage so many care-related tasks that they "feel like a general contractor" when it comes to addressing their healthcare needs.
- The complexity of billing and cost-sharing relationships is confusing to most individual consumers. "People may understand differences in plan premiums, but evidence shows many have a hard time evaluating out-of-pocket spending, a calculation that requires consumers to understand plans' cost-sharing structures and predict the amount and kind of care their household is likely to use." (Budrys 2019, p. 41)
- The transactional relationship between patient and provider is complicated by the patient's emotional needs and fears, often leading patients to demand more or less care than their physical condition necessitates. (Stoline 1988)
- Patients as consumers behave differently when shopping for healthcare than they do other commodities. "Consumers of healthcare are primarily interested in improving their health, not in getting healthcare bargains." (Budrys 2019, p. 18)

☞ **The "product" patients are buying is a clean bill of health, for which bargain-basement deals are not preferred.**

Bad News: Diagnosis and Debt

👉 **Healthcare professionals now deliver bad news to patients not only pertaining to disease, but about the cost of treating it.**

"Mr S takes you aside after his wife enters the chemotherapy room. 'Doctor, how much longer is this going to continue? We already sold our house, but the 20% copay on our $14,000-a-month chemotherapy bills (paclitaxel, carboplatin, trastuzamab, and pamidronate) are adding up quickly. I'm glad she's doing OK, but do you think she'll last another 3 months? A year? I don't mean to sound morbid, but I need to plan.'"   (McFarlane et al. 2008)

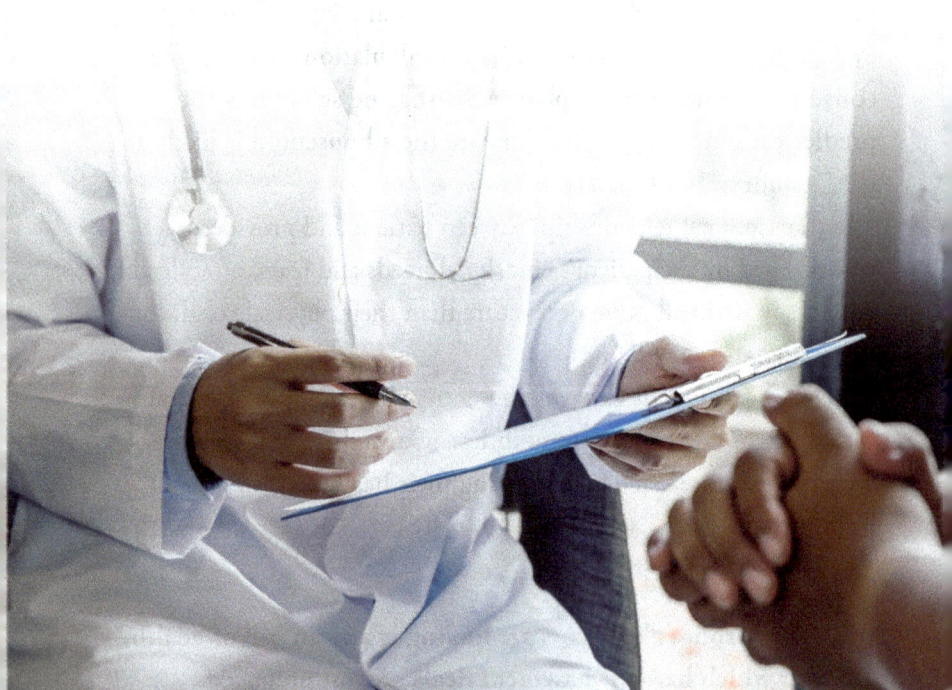

Are The Worried Well Driving Up Costs?

In 1970, Kaiser Permanente physician Sidney Garfield suggested that, owing to the affordability of healthcare provided by Medicare and Medicaid, increasing numbers of "worried well" patients were flooding clinics, seeking medical advice when they might not be clinically sick. This behavior increased costs and clogged the system for others in need of care. (Garfield 1970)

Kaiser Permanente, a Health Maintenance Organization that runs on a prepayment membership model, proposed a solution to this by expanding preventive healthcare education and devising a "multiphasic screening" protocol to direct patients to an appropriate caregiver.

The Internet Presents Quantity Over Quality

While "consumers" of healthcare would benefit from being more informed in their choices, searching the internet often has negative effects. Early on, physicians observed an increase in queries from the "worried well" who had consulted Dr. Google for diagnosis. (Powell et al. 2003) Researchers have devised a "Cyberchondria Severity Scale" to determine the impact of internet searches on diseases on health anxiety, showing the complications that arise from information proliferation without expert medical mediation. (Blackburn et al. 2019)

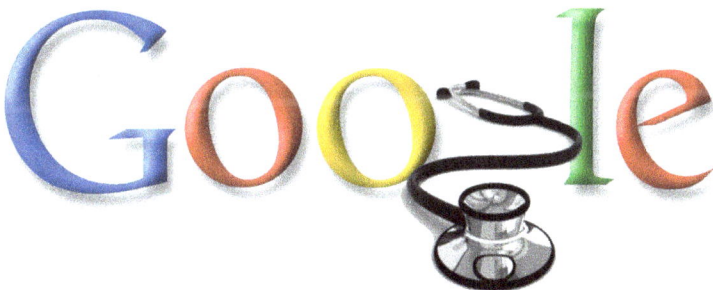

Blame the Patient????

All these commercials for things I'm told to ask my doctor about make me worried that I'm probably sick. I think it's a good idea to get some tests to make sure I'm good.

Sucker! You're a worried well person. You don't need unnecessary tests. Getting them just racks up medical bills. The US consistently spends more on healthcare per capita than any other developed country!

But isn't there's a benefit to testing and preventive screening before the hidden problems get out of control?

Look, screening recs are based on epidemiological data for specific risk groups. Check out Friedson's discussion of "flat of the curve" spending. There's a point at which healthcare spending stops improving health outcomes. Excessive testing sucks cash out of our wallets but doesn't improve health.

But healthcare providers seem perfectly happy to do the tests ...

That's probably a result of being historically conditioned to practice defensive medicine. They don't want to be sued if anything is missed, and it's all about billable hours ... check out the book by Shannon Brownlee on how we're being **overtreated.**

You're a fount of knowledge!
   Hey phone, what are the references mentioned here?

Andrew Friedson, *Economics of Healthcare: A Brief Introduction* (Cambridge: Cambridge University Press, 2023)
Brownlee, Shannon. *Overtreated: Why Too Much Medicine is Making Us Sicker and Poorer* (New York: Bloomsbury, 2008)

Do Patients Have an Incentive to Reduce Healthcare Costs?

Typically, patients want to spend as little of their own money as possible. Their healthcare costs are often mysterious and are frequently masked by insurance coverage and payment systems that can make some healthcare look inexpensive. At the same time, ever less generous coverage and payment by insurers puts more of the total cost burden on patients, who see their personal costs rising steadily.

According to one analysis, "Because patients may not value healthcare as a service in which they are willing to invest their own money upfront, they have little incentive to actively participate in reducing costs. Patients may be reluctant, for example, to make a dietary change to reduce cholesterol levels when a once-daily pill can achieve the same results." (Branning and Vater 2016) However, while out-of-pocket co-pays were found to help mitigate overuse, subsequent studies found that personal wealth is an important determinant of the use of healthcare: the richer the patient, the more services consumed, regardless of insurance policies. (Nyman 1999)

Over the last 50 years, people have felt that health insurance was inadequate. A study conducted by Harvard Opinion Research Program of more than 100 public opinion surveys done between 1950 and 2000 found dissatisfaction with private health insurance and managed care, and broad support for a national health plan. (Calvo et al. 2017)

As discussed in Chapter 4, employer-sponsored health insurance became a way for companies to attract employees in a mid-century competitive labor market. But what about those who were not employed, or self-employed, or retired? These individuals are incentivized to seek lower healthcare costs, but an individual has little power to lower healthcare costs other than to vote for government intervention.

In Summary …

Individuals' choices and behaviors can contribute to the rising costs of healthcare in several ways. The major factors that can be attributed to patients themselves can be summarized as:

→ **Overutilization of Services**. Patients sometimes demand unnecessary tests, procedures, or medications because they believe that "more care is better care." Overuse can also result from patients getting care without clear medical indications, which drives up costs without clear health benefits.

→ **Underuse of Services:** The failure to use effective and affordable medical interventions is responsible for substantial suffering, disability, and loss of life worldwide. Glasziou, et al. and other studies have shown that underuse occurs side-by-side with overuse and has a lot of variability across conditions and nations.(Glasziou, et al. 2017)

→ **Lifestyle Choices**. Poor diet, lack of exercise, tobacco use, and other unhealthy behaviors can lead to chronic diseases like heart disease, diabetes, and obesity. Treating these preventable conditions costs the healthcare system billions annually.

→ **Insurance-First Mentality**. Because many Americans have increasingly relied on third-party payers (insurance companies) covering the bulk of their healthcare expenses, there may be a reduced incentive for individuals to consider cost when seeking care.

➢   **Limited Health Literacy.** A lack of understanding health issues and the healthcare system can lead to inefficient use of services. For instance, individuals might not understand how to manage their conditions, leading to complications and higher costs down the line.

➢   **Demand for New Technologies and Treatments.** While innovation drives many positive outcomes in healthcare, the desire for the "latest and greatest" treatments or technologies—regardless of their cost-effectiveness—can contribute to higher costs.

➢   **Voting Against Healthcare Reforms.** Despite an overwhelming majority of US citizens believing that healthcare is in crisis, is too costly, and is controlled by special interests, government intervention has historically been kept at bay by voters. The Affordable Care Act (2010) and piecemeal legislative measures such as the CARES Act (2020) and Inflation Reduction Act (2022) are exceptions.

2

Physicians

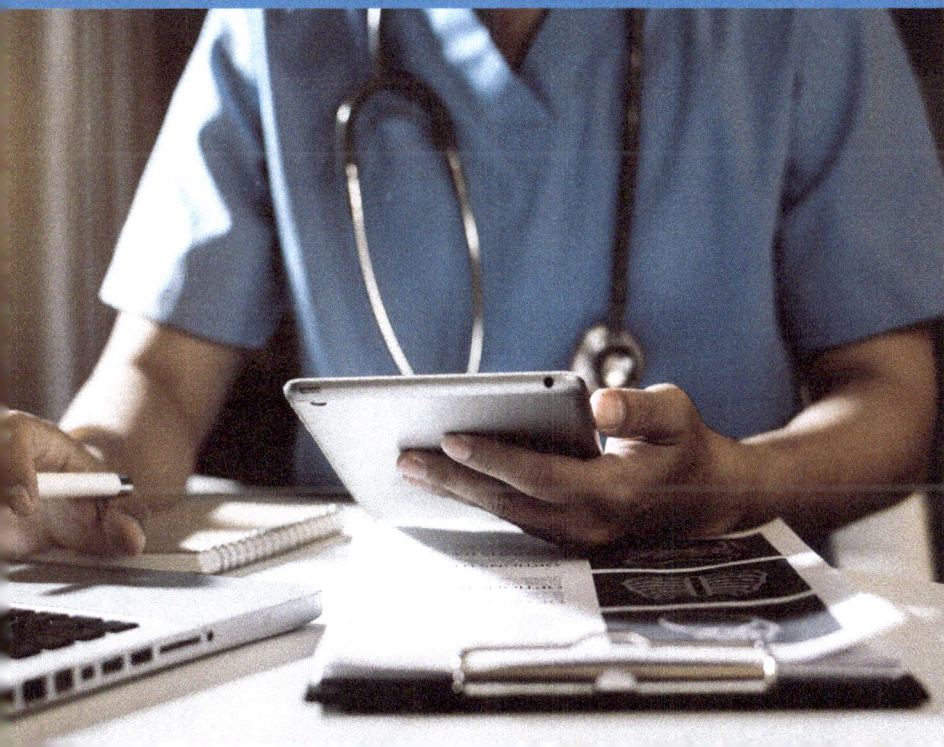

Physicians and other providers attribute the high costs of healthcare to circumstances outside their control, often not knowing what hospitals will charge or what insurance covers.

Why It Matters

Physicians are fighting against a "pandemic of mistrust" in medicine that partly lies in a public perception that physicians themselves are responsible for driving up healthcare costs. The challenge facing the profession is that history lends support to this assertion. (Harmon 2022)

Why Healthcare Is Expensive According to Doctors

- Administrative costs linked to increased staffing to navigate a complicated world of insurance plans, hospital fees, and regulations
- Rising costs of equipment that cater to the "technological imperative" to use whatever resources are available to diagnose and treat disease
- The high cost of prescription drugs set by the pharmaceutical industry
- The need to manage long-term, chronic diseases often linked to patient lifestyle factors (e.g., diabetes, heart disease, COPD)

However, there is also a finger that points to the profession itself:
- For Medicare reimbursements, the government agreed to pay "customary and reasonable fees" established by the profession which work in the interests of high physician pay

Most accounts of American healthcare since the 1970s describe its fragmentation, inefficiencies, run-away costs, impersonal care, uneven distribution, variable quality, and over-specialization, but without acknowledging how these emanated from a professionally driven healthcare system operating in its own professionally constructed markets." (Light 2004, p. 14)

A Cost Conundrum

Can Doctors Be Frugal?

Dr. Arnold S. Relman, editor of the *New England Journal of Medicine* (1977-1991) and fierce critic of the for-profit healthcare industry, wrote in 1983 of "an internal moral crisis" facing physicians. Physicians are, he said, "no different from other citizens. They have the same strengths and weaknesses of character and are susceptible to the same economic temptations as anyone else. What gives physicians special influence is the trust reposed in them by the public and the responsibility for the care of their patients invested in them by law." (Relman 1985)

Does this trust translate into efficient care? In the 1980s, the government introduced the Prospective Payment System (PPS) as a means of reimbursing hospitals for Medicare patients, where reimbursement was fixed and was based on the disease category into which a patient's problem fell. Yet doctors continued to be paid on a fee-for-service arrangement, so that the longer a patient remained in a hospital and received services, the more the physician earned, but not the hospital where expenses related to inpatient admission continued to grow. Could doctors be given incentives to be frugal in their decisions? Or would this compromise the quality of care?

By The Numbers

Who has a "major responsibility" for reducing health-care costs?

The percentage of doctors from 2,556 respondents of a survey (2012) thought the following:

- **trial lawyers (60%)**
- **health insurance companies (59%)**
- **hospitals and health systems (56%)**
- **pharmaceutical and device manufacturers (56%)**
- **patients (52%)**

Whereas only 36% reported that practicing physicians have a major responsibility for reducing healthcare costs. (Tilburt et al. 2013)

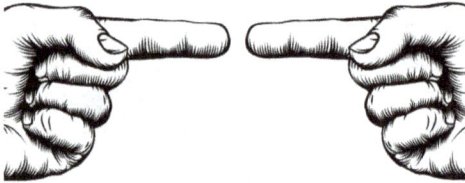

Reflecting on how their practice affects costs:

- 76% were aware of the costs of the tests/treatments they recommend
- 79% agreed that they should adhere to clinical guidelines that discourage the use of marginally beneficial care
- 89% agreed that doctors need to take a more prominent role in limiting use of unnecessary tests (Tilburt et al. 2013)

On Discussing Costs

One thousand randomly selected physicians in five northern California counties responded to a survey in 2000. It showed that most physicians regard cost-effectiveness as an appropriate component of clinical decisions and think that only the treating physician and patient should decide what is cost-worthy. "However, physicians are divided on whether they have a duty to offer medical interventions with remote chances of benefit regardless of cost, and they vary considerably in their interactions with patients when cost-effectiveness is an issue." (Ginsburg et al. 2000, p. 390)

In 2016, 333 physicians responded to a survey. 60% reported addressing costs frequently or always in clinic, 40% addressed costs rarely or never, and 36% did not believe it is the doctor's responsibility to explain costs of care to patients. "Few [responding physicians] believe they have adequate resources to discuss costs, suggesting that greater cost transparency, education concerning costs of care, tools to facilitate discussions, and validated interventions are needed." (Altomare et al. 2016, 247)

Fee-For-Service Allows Greater Control Over Professional Income

Why It Matters

The US healthcare system largely operates on a fee-for-service model, which means providers are paid for each test, procedure, or visit. Critics, including some physicians, argue that this can incentivize overuse of services, as payment is tied to quantity rather than necessity of care.

The US Healthcare Finance Administration estimated that inflation of physician fees in excess of general inflation was responsible for 15 percent of the total growth in expenditures for medical services from the beginning of Medicare in 1966 to 1984. (Stoline and Weiner 1988)

While the medical marketplace has diversified greatly since 1980 with the rise of HMOs and other cooperative healthcare plans, physician fees have generally continued to outpace inflation. Between 1980 and 2007, prices paid by urban consumers (reflecting 87% of the US population) for medical care outpaced the overall Consumer Price Index (CPI). (Stewart 2008)

	PRIVATE 1DAYS	2124.00	2124.00	2124.00
R&C PRIVATE 28DAYS	2141.00	59948.00	59948.00
PHARMACY		135870.52	
			135870.52
SUPPLY/DEVICES		1618.00	1618.00
LAB		24889.17	24889.17
LAB/PATH		1799.00	1799.00
RADIOLOGY/DX		630.00	630.00
CT SCAN		6471.00	6471.00
OPERATING ROOM		1488.00	1488.00
BLOOD PROCESS FEE		1823.69	1823.69
IMAGING SERV		631.00	631.00
CARDIOLOGY		1869.00	1869.00
MRI		6314.00	6314.00
MED/SURG SUPPLY		250.00	250.00
OTHER		3465.00	3465.00

The Use of Ambulatory Testing in Prepaid and Fee-for-Service Group Practices

Arnold M. Epstein, M.D., M.A., Colin B. Begg, Ph.D., and Barbara J. McNeil, M.D., Ph.D.

Article   Figures/Media

April 24, 1986
N Engl J Med 1986; 314:1089-1094
DOI: 10.1056/NEJM198604243141706

23 References   50 Citing Articles   Letters

Abstract

To examine the influence of method of payment on ambulatory testing by internists, we compared the rate at which patients with uncomplicated hypertension were tested by 10 doctors practicing in large fee-for-service groups with that by 17 doctors in large prepaid groups. We examined the use of individual tests and asked the doctors in the fee-for-service groups what they believed about the profitability and costs of tests.

After correcting for the patient's age, sex, duration of disease, and severity of disease as measured by pretreatment blood pressure, and for the doctor's year of medical school graduation, we found that 50 percent more electrocardiograms were obtained among patients in fee-for-service practices (0.69 per patient per year vs. 0.45, P = 0.006), and 40 percent more chest radiographs (0.49 vs. 0.35, P = 0.11). Fee-for-service doctors believed that both tests were associated with high profit and costs.

These results suggest that the use of certain high-profit, high-cost tests is higher in large fee-for-service groups than in large prepaid groups. Although the generalizability of conclusions based on this limited study must be considered tentative, the findings suggest that it may be appropriate to consider changing the payments for tests as part of a more general reform of the fee schedules. (N Engl J Med 1986; 314:1089–94.)

Does fee-for-service payment nudge doctors to increase the amount of services they charged for?

A study of how many diagnostic tests a group of fee-for-service (FFS) physicians ordered compared their behavior with a group of prepaid-plan (such as HMOs) physicians. The study found that the FFS practitioners ordered 40-50% more tests than HMO practitioners when dealing with comparable samples of patients. (Epstein et al. 1986)

Keyword: "Demand Inducement"

Economists have theorized that physicians have an inducement to increase demand for services for which they are reimbursed, and this increases the cost of medical care. A corollary motto for hospital administrators was, "A bed built is a bed filled," based on observations in the 1960s that increased capacity led to increased admissions, even though the smaller hospital was not completely full. (Dranove 2000)

Demanding Fee-For-Service and Prohibiting Consumer-Sponsored Health Plans Turns Out To Be Illegal

In the 1930s and '40s, medical societies routinely expelled physicians who worked in prepaid programs operated by consumer cooperatives and labor unions. Doctors needed medical society membership to keep their licenses and hospital privileges. Courts found that this was a violation of the Sherman Antitrust Act of 1890.

In the 1942 case *American Medical Association v. United States*, 130 F.2d 233 (D.C. Cir. 1942), the United States Court of Appeals for the District of Columbia Circuit affirmed that the AMA was guilty of obstructing consumer-sponsored health plans. The court held that this conduct constituted a restraint of trade, which was a violation of antitrust laws, and ruled that "health is too important to be wholly trusted to the doctors." (Ward 1989)

The antitrust act prohibits physicians and healthcare providers (among other professions) from engaging in price-fixing or collusion. For example, physicians can't agree with each other to set the fees they will charge patients or insurers. A lawsuit filed against the American Medical Association by the Federal Trade Commission (FTC) in 1975 affirmed that the professional organization's prohibition on advertising violated antitrust laws by limiting competition.

"Physician autonomy has been a defining feature of our health economy for nearly the entire century. Prior to the 1980s, virtually all physicians had a solo practice or belonged to a small group." (Dranove 2000, p. 19)

Are HMOs Unethical? The AMA Thought So

Up until the 1970s, the medical profession was largely immune to charges of monopoly in the marketplace. The assumption was that physicians were protected from commercial pressures and conflicts of interest by the professional standards that they had developed during the nineteenth century. Those standards were based on the doctor's belief that patients were not ordinary consumers and that doctors had an ethical responsibility to regulate their own behavior. The ethical guidelines asserted that such self-regulation could be jeopardized if medical practice fell under corporate control. (Dolan and Beitler 2022)

During the lengthy legal battle between the FTC and the American Medical Association (AMA) in the 1970s and 1980s, one of the central issues was the AMA's ethical guidelines, which, according to the FTC, restricted physicians from participating in certain kinds of contractual relationships, notably prepaid health plans (an early form of health maintenance organizations or HMOs). The AMA maintained that:

> *investor owned care embodies a new value system that severs the communal roots and Samaritan traditions of hospitals, makes doctors and nurses the instruments of investors, and views patients as commodities."*

Callahan and Wasunna 2006, p. 46)

The AMA defended its opposition to prepaid plans and salaried arrangements for physicians based on several arguments that were framed in terms of medical ethics and patient care.

These included:

- **Quality of Care**: Salaried positions or prepaid plans might create financial incentives for physicians to provide less than optimal care (e.g., by minimizing the time spent with each patient or avoiding costly treatments).
- **Physician Autonomy and Independent Judgment**: Being employees of a larger organization could place physicians in a position where business considerations, rather than medical judgment, dictated patient care. (Woolhander and Himmelstein 1995)
- **Patient Choice**: Prepaid health plans could limit patients' ability to choose their physician.
- **Conflict of Interest**: Compensation might be tied to the financial performance of the plan or organization, rather than to the outcomes of medical services. This, they argued, could compromise the physician's primary duty to the patient.

It's important to note that while the AMA framed these arguments in terms of ethics and patient care, the FTC and the courts ultimately found that the effect of the AMA's ethical guidelines was to restrain competition in violation of antitrust laws.

When the courts ruled with the FTC, the AMA was forced to change its ethical guidelines, which opened the door to wider acceptance and growth of HMOs and other prepaid health plans, which have become a significant part of the US healthcare landscape.

How the Courts Viewed the AMA's Ethics Argument

In 1978, the Federal Trade Commission filed a complaint against the American Medical Association alleging that the AMA prevented physicians from engaging in alternative arrangements to the traditional fee-for-service practice, such as prepaid health plans (an early form of health maintenance organizations, or HMOs).

The case was a significant legal battle, and in 1982, an administrative law judge ruled in favor of the FTC, holding that the AMA's actions were an unreasonable restraint on competition and violated federal antitrust law.

The case eventually went to the US Supreme Court, which, in a 1982 decision (American Medical Association v. FTC, 455 U.S. 676), upheld the FTC's authority to regulate the professional conduct of doctors through its general authority to regulate "commerce."

In 1983, the FTC issued a final order finding that the AMA's ethical guidelines did, in fact, unreasonably restrain competition among physicians and between physicians and non-physician providers. The AMA was prohibited from restricting its members from engaging in advertising or from participating in HMOs, preferred provider organizations (PPOs), or other salaried positions.

This case was **a significant milestone in the development of competition in healthcare** in the United States, as it effectively removed some barriers to the development and expansion of HMOs and other non-fee-for-service healthcare arrangements. (Coombs 2005)

Variations in Healthcare Practices Cost Money

Variations in medical practice refer to differences in the care provided by different physicians or hospitals to patients with the same condition. They can be significant and can exist across regions, among hospitals within the same region, and even among doctors in the same hospital. Variations can result from differences in professional opinion, patient population, availability of services, financial incentives, and other factors.

Why It Matters

Variable or inconsistent healthcare practices lead patients to believe that the lack of coordination among various healthcare providers generates redundant or unnecessary services, which can increase costs. They're often right. Lack of shared data about best practices fails to promote efficiencies.

But it's clinical judgment!

The medical profession has historically celebrated the embodiment of incommunicable diagnostic skills and clinical experienc to make medical decisions, resisting the formulas of "cookbook medicine" that might be seen to dictate actions. Others see this paternalism over evidence-based practice. (Montgomery 2006)

Variations in practice result in unequal health outcomes across different patient groups and can affect costs in a number of ways:

→ **Overuse of Services**: Some physicians may order more tests, prescribe more drugs, or perform more procedures than are medically necessary, increasing healthcare costs.

→ **Ignoring Cheaper Alternatives to Expensive Services**: Some doctors may prefer newer medications or devices, even when older, less expensive alternatives are just as effective.

→ **Lack of Standardization**: When every doctor or hospital does things a bit differently, it becomes difficult to identify best practices and encourage providers to follow them, which can lead to inefficiencies and increased costs.

→ **Defensive Medicine**: Some doctors may order extra tests and procedures to protect themselves from potential malpractice lawsuits, not because they believe the tests are medically necessary.

→ **Fragmentation of Care**: When patients receive care from multiple providers who may not communicate well with each other (a situation more likely to occur in the absence of standardized practices), it can lead to redundant testing and treatments.

→ **Administrative Burden**: Dealing with myriad treatment regimens and billing practices across healthcare systems, insurers, and hospitals is less efficient.   (Phelps and Mooney 1993)

Historical Vignette: The Study that Stimulated Health Outcomes Research

The seminal research of John Wennberg, a physician from Harvard Medical School, and Alan Gittelsohn, a biostatistician from Johns Hopkins University, has had a profound impact on health services research, specifically in understanding variations in medical practice and their implications for healthcare quality, outcomes, and costs. Their pioneering studies highlighted significant geographic variations in healthcare delivery and utilization, which could not be explained by variation in patient illness or preferences.

In the 1970s, Wennberg and Gittelsohn published a series of articles that showed great variation in utilization of healthcare services among 193 small areas distributed over six states in New England, despite the populations being similar in socio-economic status, ethnic background, health insurance coverage, and the distribution of reported illnesses. A culmination of their work was published in *Scientific American* in 1982, where they summarized their findings by saying that the amount and cost of hospital treatment in any particular community had less to do with the health of the population being treated and more to do with the "style of practice" adopted by physicians. Physicians in certain areas appeared to conform to local practice standards that resulted in far higher rates of medical interventions, such as hysterectomies. (Wennberg and Gittelsohn 1982)

The obvious question was: did different practice standards produce different health outcomes? **Health services research** takes this as a foundational question that led to promoting evidence-based practice, and improving the efficiency and effectiveness of healthcare delivery.

Medical Specialization Creates Specialized Costs

The number of medical specialists soared in the post-World War II era when training programs expanded and new drugs and technologies emerged. By the 1960s and 1970s, the number of physicians choosing to specialize had increased dramatically, and specialists had become a prominent and established part of the medical profession, eclipsing the numbers of general practitioners. (Bartz 2005) This aligned with a shift in where medical care was delivered, away from general practice in solo or small-group practices towards health organizations, hospital-based practice, and specialized clinics. This made it more practical and desirable for physicians to specialize. Cost-wise, this resulted in:

→ **Higher fees**: Specialized medical professionals often command higher salaries due to the extended education and training they undergo.

→ **Expensive tools**: Specialization typically involves the use of advanced, often expensive, technology and equipment.

CARDIOLOGY PATHOLOGY DERMOTOXICOLOGY PNEUMOLOGY MICROBIOLOGY NEUROPHYSIOLOGY UROLOGY ENDOCRINOLOGY ALLERGY AND IMMUNOLOGY RADIOLOGY PATHOLOGY SURGERY PEDIATRICS NEPHROLOGY OPHTHALMOLOGY PSYCHOLOGY GERIATRICS OBSTETRICS ORTHOPAEDICS OTORHINOLARYGOLOGY

Complex Healthcare Settings Are Costly to Manage

Physicians have historically used hospitals as an extension of their private practices, increasingly requiring access to specialized areas of care and expensive equipment. However, they also demand autonomy in decision making and control over their working environment, sometimes putting them at odds with hospital administrators and insurers.

What emerged was an inherent tension between physicians and hospitals regarding the costs associated with patient care.

Hospitals are independent corporations who grant physicians "privileges" to use the facility, which is governed by boards protecting their interests.

With increasing complexities involved in billing, obtaining utilization review approval for procedures, and dealing with a myriad of reimbursement rules, physicians started hiring teams of nonmedical administrators. By the 1990s, according to health economist David Dranove, "many physicians have stopped trying to run the business side of their practice altogether and have sold their practice assets and a share of their practice (usually 15 percent) to physician practice management (PPM) firms." (Dranove 2000, p. 105) Outsourcing helps physicians focus on their core practice responsibilities but shifting administrative duties to outside firms is costly.

These increased costs facing physicians are ultimately shouldered by patients, whose point of view places much of the blame on hospital administration, which is examined in the next chapter.

3

Hospitals

> *In 1929, only 18 percent of the healthcare dollar was spent in hospitals; by 1965, this had risen to about 34 percent. Since the passage of Medicaid and Medicare, the portion of the healthcare dollar spent in hospitals has moved to 40 percent.*"
>
> (Barocci 1981, p. 23)

According to the National Health Expenditure Data from the Centers for Medicare & Medicaid Services (CMS), in 2019, hospital care spending accounted for 37% of total healthcare in the US, the largest percentage of personal health expenditure.

But watch this space: in 2022 the portion of the healthcare dollar spent in hospitals was 30%, reflecting slower growth in spending by Medicare and Medicaid. However, it remains the largest percent of overall healthcare expenditure, over physician services (20%) and retail drugs (9%).

Throughout The Twentieth Century, Hospitals Grew In Dominance As Sites Of Care

Why It Matters

This has resulted in more capital building costs, administrative expenses, and complex services for patients, the costs of which are not controlled by conventional market forces. Hospitals often defy market economics because of the highly varied services or "products" that they provide to consumers who lack knowledge about what they are buying. Patients frequently don't know, through no fault of their own, that they are agreeing to buy something until the bill arrives.

"For-profit hospitals, because of [costly up-front] entry barriers, information asymmetry, and the ambiguity of the physician's role as the consumer's agent, may not be presumed to produce the quantity and quality of services desired by society at an efficient price." (Gray 1986, p. 24)

By the mid-twentieth century, almost all industrialized nations adopted some form of publicly controlled healthcare system, believing that healthcare is a public good that should be facilitated by the government. Not so in the US, where free market economic principles were applied to control costs. (Porter 1999)

Keyword: "Information Asymmetry"

When consumers are at an informational disadvantage, the market may not provide sufficient discipline to prevent a for-profit producer from marketing inferior services at excessive prices. (Hansmann 1979; Steinberg and Gray. 1993)

Hospitals Organized As Corporations and Operated With the Goal of Generating a Profit For Their Shareholders

Why It Matters

A common assumption is that for-profit systems will create bias toward high-profit services and neglect quality or range of services that are required of a diverse community of consumers.

In addition, economic analysts have observed that for-profit hospitals fail to reach optimal efficiencies or attain a level of consumer satisfaction that a competitive market model predicts, allowing high costs to prevail in a uniquely complex industry. (Jeurissen, et. al. 2021)

Hospitals Are Charitable, Right?

"They were 'charities' in terms of the sources from which they drew money for buildings and other capital investments. Capital came almost entirely from private gifts, endowments, and donations until after World War Two … In terms of day-to-day operations, however, the early 20th - century hospital was more like a business." (Stevens 1989, p. 33)

Americans have tolerated a healthcare system that leaves millions without adequate coverage based on the belief that a medical safety net exists in the form of hospitals that provide charity care—public hospitals owned by the government, academic, or faith-based nonprofit hospitals. (Cohn 2007, p. 143)

Historical Rise Of Hospital Care

Not-for-profit (mainly religious or charitable) hospitals became the dominant model of community care in the 1920s and 1930s, and continue to control the majority of beds nationwide today. Yet, for-profit hospitals are not new. In the early 1900s more than half of the hospitals in the United States were proprietary.

The first wave of hospital growth occurred in the 1920s. "Between 1925 and 1929, $890 million was spent on the construction of hospitals and related institutions, almost 80% more than was spent between 1921 and 1924," according to historian Rosemary Stevens. "This investment made hospitals one of the largest enterprises in the United States, outstripped only by the iron and steel industry, the textile industry, the chemical industry, and the food industry." (Stevens 1989, p. 111)

A second expansion of hospitals followed the passage of the Hospital Survey and Construction Act (known as the Hill-Burton Act) of 1946. Over 9,000 healthcare facilities, concentrated in underserved areas, were built.

The third wave of hospital growth began in the late 1960s. The launch of investor-owned hospital companies was spurred by the rise of third-party payments for hospital care, especially through Medicare and Medicaid.

Throughout the 1960s–1980s, **the rate of growth of for-profit (investor owned) hospitals exceeded nonprofit systems**, with the majority of these new hospitals controlled by four major companies, concentrated in states with the greatest increases in per capita income and population, with widespread insurance coverage. (Gray 1986, 29)

Cost Efficiency Was Attempted by Making Patients Units of Mass Production

Why It Matters

For a hospital to be strong economically, administrators need performance measures that reflect the hospital's efficiency at healthcare delivery. Inspired by "Fordism," or the success of early American mass-production led by Henry Ford, hospitals were re-conceptualized as factories, with accountable units of inputs and outputs. This led to the commodification of patient care and the notion that hospitals could be successful for-profit, corporate entities.

The Making of the Hospital Factory

In a "typical" hospital, the cost of maintaining one patient for one day rose from $2.65 in 1919 to $4.71 in 1928, an increase of nearly 80%. (Caldwell 1930, p. 4) Even in these early days attempts were made to slow rising costs by identifying and measuring the appropriate "inputs" necessary for the hospital to produce successful "outputs"—treated patients. But how is success measured?

As America's industrial capacity grew rapidly between 1875 and 1900, questions about the best ways to manage growing hospitals arose. One approach in the early twentieth century was made by the New England surgeon Ernest Amory Codman, who devised what he called the "End Result System," a first-of-its kind quality assurance program that tracked patients long enough after treatment to determine whether the treatment worked, and if not, to collect data on why not. "A factory," Codman said, "takes pains to assure itself that the product is a good one, but the hospital does not. It is the hospital's duty to do so." (Codman 1914; Reverby 1981, p. 162)

Physicians and professional organizations such as the American Medical Association pushed back, arguing that clinical judgment was more beneficial than "cookbook" care because each patient was different. However, sixty years later, Codman's ideas saw a renaissance with the emergence of corporate-owned hospital systems, which reinvigorated the study of the "product of a hospital," as corporate ownership placed renewed emphasis on performance efficiency.

"The output of a hospital/firm is patient care, and the inputs are services and goods supplied by departments within the hospital that have a functional orientation," explained Thomas Barocci, professor of economics at MIT in the 1970s. (Barocci 1981, p. 76)

How Physicians Became Cogs in the Hospital Factory Wheel

The management of inputs shifted to hospital administrators. Whereas the physician once controlled the inputs (i.e., resources necessary to provide treatment) based on their assessment of the needs of the patient, the explosion of technologies and treatment options made this increasingly complicated, burdened by high capital investment costs and specialized training that became too much for small clinical practices.

Yet, here's the crux: "Hospitals do not compete for patients; they compete for doctors who compete for patients. A hospital competes for doctors by offering the latest, best, and most extensive medical facilities, equipment, support staff, and prestige." (Barocci 1981, p. 82)

Faced with the impracticality of physicians managing the system of hospital care and the rising concern about healthcare costs, the administrators found themselves party to a conflict: offer the services and goods to provide the care prescribed by physicians, but deliver under the pressures of fiscal and regulatory constraints.

Regulatory constraints? For example, owing to the high cost of medical technologies, in 1974 the government began requiring a "**certificate of need**," a justification *for the use* of the technology a hospital desired to purchase (but not to provide a justification for *the cost* of the technology). Therefore, unless there was a compelling case against the benefits of having a medical technology, its purchase could be justified on the basis of its benefit being greater than zero. (Russell 1979; National Health Planning and Resources Development Act 1974)

The Growth of For-Profit Hospitals Established a New Model of Economic Management

"It is difficult to overstate the hostility with which the mainstream healthcare community reacted to the success of the investor-owned systems." (Dranove 2000, p. 59)

Why It Matters

Investors saw a growth industry and transformed the medical marketplace through aggressive acquisition and consolidation of smaller hospitals and expanded beds to maximize output. This raised public concern about whether shareholder interests were prioritized over public good.

The expansion of available beds created demand inducement and overutilization, increasing healthcare expenses. Milton Roemer, a physician and health policy researcher, found a direct correlation between the number of hospital beds in a given area and the use of those beds. "**Roemer's Law**" accordingly states that an available hospital bed is an occupied hospital bed; the supply creates the demand. (Stoline and Weiner 1988, p. 51)

"the coming of the corporation"
- Sociologist Paul Starr on the heyday of for-profit hospital expansion (1982)

"medical-industrial complex"
- Arnold Relman, editor of NEJM, warning of the corporate-driven healthcare arms race (1980)

The Money Motive

A number of assumptions about the management of for-profit versus nonprofit hospitals reflect expectations of how each impacts overall healthcare costs. Broadly speaking, they are framed by the following dichotomies:

- That **for-profit** hospitals might increase costs in their quest to return greater profit to investors, or …
- **For-profit** hospitals might reach economies of scale to reduce expenditures and therefore return better margins of profit for investors.

- That **nonprofit** hospitals concentrate more on community care to meet their charitable mission, and therefore would not drive-up costs, or …
- **Nonprofit** systems find it difficult to sustain their mission through philanthropy and borrowed money, raising concerns that repaying debt becomes a priority, beholding them to bondholders the way for-profits are to shareholders.

What is the Difference Between a Nonprofit and For-Profit Hospital?

The two are often indistinguishable in terms of their operations—they both have professional management, negotiate aggressively with insurers, and focus on expanding profitable lines of service. The main difference is their tax status, with nonprofits needing to meet requirements to provide some level of community benefit in exchange for that status.

TABLE: DISTINGUISHING FOR-PROFIT V. NONPROFIT

FOR-PROFIT	NONPROFIT

• Owned by corporations or investors
• Distribute profits to owners
• Generate income through:
    Equity capital from investors
    Debt
    Retained earnings
 	
Mission to grow the organization, implement efficiencies, and enhance the wealth of shareholders
	• Owned by nonprofit organizations or charities
	• Must redistribute surplus revenue to support services
	• Generally exempt from taxes
	• Generate income through:
	    Philanthropy
	    Debt
	    Government grants
	
	Mission oriented toward charitable service and community care

👉 10% of Americans carry medical debt; 75% of them owe some, or all of it, to hospitals (Karpman 2023)

Despite what one may think ...

Nonprofit Hospitals Rely Less On Philanthropy and More on Debt Financing

Why It Matters

Federal laws require nonprofit hospitals to have financial assistance policies and eligibility requirements for charity care, though such policies are determined by hospitals and often result in patient debt.

Hospitals can sell that debt to collections agencies, or sue patients to collect outstanding debt. Hospitals can sometimes write off uncollected medical debt as charity care, allowing nonprofits to meet the conditions of tax exemption.

In the 1970s, nonprofit hospital financing took a turn away from the philanthropic endowment model to debt financing (borrowing money). By 1975 two-thirds of all capital raised by hospitals was debt.

(Barocci 1981, p. 89)

Studies Found That For-Profit Hospitals Were Less Effective at Controlling Costs Than Nonprofit Hospitals

→ Data analyzed from the 1980s found that cost to payers (patients, insurers) for care at for-profit hospitals was 15-25% higher than costs at not-for-profit hospitals. (Gray 1986, pp. 80-84)

→ A study that examined data from 1970s to 1990s concluded that administrative costs were higher (exceeding 30% of total operating costs) in for-profit systems. (Woolhandler and Himmelstein 1997)

→ For-profit systems faced an expense disadvantage in part because of low occupancy rates; they were providing staff wages to care for fewer patients.

→ In 1983, when overall US hospital occupancy was 73%, for-profit hospitals had occupancy rates of around 63%, whereas occupancy rates of nonprofit hospitals was approximately 75%.

Historical Vignette: Merger Mania and the Great Debate Over Market Power and Hospital Pricing

In his 1991 book *The Profit Motive and Patient Care*, Bradford Gray, professor of public health at Yale University, questioned whether the rapid expansion of corporate-owned hospital systems would uphold the ideals of community service, maintain public trust, and perform to professional standards expected of healthcare providers. Up to the 1960s, he noted, the idealistic image of paternalistic physicians providing care in small, benevolent practices for public good, was being eroded by the public experience of astronomically high healthcare costs. Whereas the profession had traditionally relied on the "physician fiduciary ethic" (always acting in the interests of the patient and having no conflict of interest), physicians were increasingly accountable to large organizations with economic interests at play.

Yet other authors exalted competitive economic forces of an open market as a solution to controlling healthcare costs. In 1995, Sandy Lutz and E. Preston Gee published *The For-Profit Healthcare Revolution*, arguing that "the individual market will determine the most effective structure" of healthcare services. The position puts full faith in corporate performance, going as far as claiming that, "Like shares of IBM or futures in cotton, hospitals are now a commodity ..." (Lutz and Gee 1995, p. 3).

In 1999, the Berkeley professor of health economics, James Robinson, published *The Corporate Practice of Medicine*, examining how hospitals mirror other corporate sectors in terms of ownership, governance, finance, compensation, and marketing. He posited that "organizational innovation" was the key to corporate survival and would solve an inherent conflict in attempts to manage healthcare costs.

Yet in 1987, Robinson and UCSF health policy professor Hal Luft found that competition *increased costs* per patient. Studying data from more than 5,000 hospitals between 1972 to 1982, they found that costs were 15 percent higher in competitive markets compared to hospitals with no neighbors. Why? "It is our hypothesis that hospitals in more competitive local environments have been forced to provide higher levels of both patient- and physician-oriented services than hospitals whose access to patients is less threatened." (Robinson and Luft 1987) This supports what Hughes and Luft (1991) subsequently characterized as the "medical arms race," where hospitals must increase their services consistently to outperform competitors, creating expenses and forcing them to raise costs.

In 1997, the Stanford professor of economics and health policy, Victor Fuchs, questioned the logic of "merger mania," pointing out that "Studies of mergers in other industries have not shown widespread cost reductions or improvements in profitability, on average." (Fuchs 1997) A 1999 study examined data on hospital mergers in 1986, 1989, 1992, and 1994 and determined "that prices at for-profit hospitals averaged 10 percent higher in 1994 than nonprofits." (Melnick et al. 1999)

In 2002 hospital costs overtook pharmaceutical costs as the major source of increasing healthcare costs. However, notwithstanding merger mania, by the 2000s the growth rate of the for-profit hospital sector levelled out, and nonprofit systems maintain the majority of beds overall. A common counter-argument to critiques of for-profit structures is simply that nonprofits are not much different, and take advantage of their tax exempt status and unregulated criteria for offering charitable care to gain their own competitive edge.

POP QUIZ: WAS THIS SENSATIONAL HEALTH-CARE INDUSTRY COLLAPSE A FOR-PROFIT OR NONPROFIT?

RESEARCH ARTICLE

HEALTH AFFAIRS > VOL. 19, NO. 1

Health Affairs

The Fall Of The House Of AHERF: The Allegheny Bankruptcy

Lawton R. Burns, John Cacciamani, James Clement, and Welman Aquino

PUBLISHED: JANUARY/FEBRUARY 2000   No Access   https://doi.org/10.1377/hlthaff.19.1.7

⬇ VIEW ARTICLE   🔒 PERMISSIONS   ≺ SHARE   🔧 TOOLS

Abstract

PROLOGUE:

The drama of the collapse of the Allegheny Health, Education, and Research Foundation (AHERF) has captured the attention of industry observers from Wall Street to the ivory towers of academe. All are eager to know who ultimately held responsibility—legal, financial, and managerial—for AHERF's decline. Part of the intrigue of the story certainly stems from the fact that so many actors, both inside and outside the company, appear to have played a part.

Historian Gabriel Winant investigated the rise, and fall, of the healthcare industry that emerged in Pennsylvania in the wake of deindustrialization. He followed the story of Allegheny Health, Education, and Research Foundation (AHERF), which from 1988 to 1996 went on an acquisition binge, buying up hospitals and medical schools across the state. "Seeking to gain market share, AHERF overextended itself disastrously, particularly by diving into the competitive Philadelphia market. Over little more than a decade, AHERF grew from 3,610 employees to 29,500, and from $ 329 million in assets to $ 2.6 billion. Then, hugely overleveraged, it collapsed in 1998 in **the largest nonprofit healthcare bankruptcy in history**." (Winant 2021)

Overexpansion Led to Economic Crisis Linked to Capital Costs and Underused Beds

Many factors drove growth in the number of hospitals, for-profit and nonprofit, after 1945 until the 1990s:

- The general growth in the US population, up from 132 million in 1940 to 203 million in 1970 (a 53% increase), led to increased demand that fueled expansion.
- After WWII the US faced a shortage of hospital beds. The Hill-Burton Act of 1946 put $3.7 billion into nonprofit hospitals for construction and improvements to provide care to underserved communities. In the 20 years after the implementation of Hill-Burton, over 5,000 short-term hospital projects were approved, adding nearly 350,000 new beds at a cost of $10 billion.
- Medical advances and new technologies increased the demand for hospital stay.
- The expansion of hospitals and increase in hospital beds was tied to increased specialization in clinical practice. Different wards, such as psychiatric or Ob/Gyn, carved out space with an allocation of beds at their control.

With the Notion of Hospitals as Factories, Bed Occupancy Became a Unit Of Production

Why It Matters

It is economically advantageous to fill an empty hospital bed with a paying patient. The revenue generated by a filled bed, combined with little pressure to shorten stays, led to concerns about overutilization and unnecessary expenses. As a check against this, **utilization review committees** were introduced.

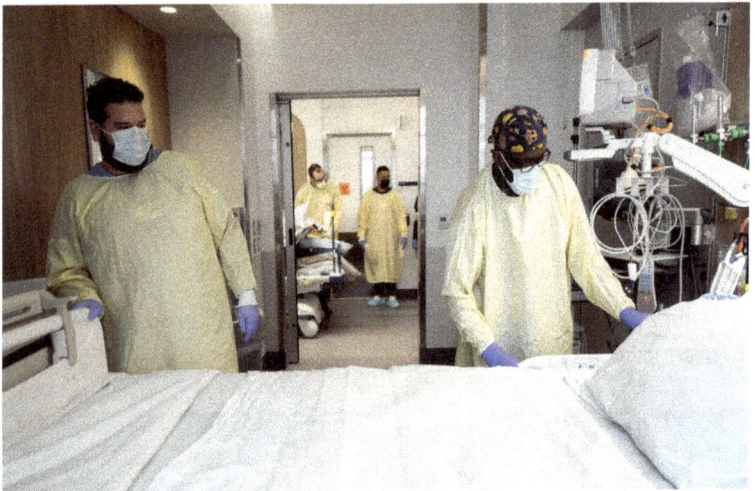

How Hospital Beds Became Cost Units

If the product of a hospital is a healthy patient, then it was useful to know how many patients a hospital can treat in order to maximize return. Since hospitals conventionally focused on in-patient or critical care, the hospital bed became a proxy for capacity, making the reference to the number of beds in a hospital a common measure of its service capacity.

The Big Picture

Throughout the twentieth century, different areas of the US had different numbers of hospital beds (calculated per 1000 people) available to provide care to that local population. In 1946, the Hill-Burton Act provided federal grants to increase the volume of service in underrepresented areas. Construction costs were based on the all-in costs needed to make that bed functional: real estate, servicing technology, staffing, facilities management, etc.

The number of beds proposed for construction was originally based on **projected utilization**, referencing current hospitalization practices. However, hospitals could portray having heavy current utilization by encouraging liberal admissions policies and prolonged stays.

As a result of the investment in, and expansion of, hospitals in the 1970s, the American healthcare system found itself with a surplus of empty beds, costing money but not generating revenue.

A study by the Institute of Medicine in 1976 recommended that a new national health planning goal be implemented under the provisions of the 1974 National Health Planning and Resources Development Act (P.L. 93-641) to **reduce short-term general hospital beds** by 10% by 1981.

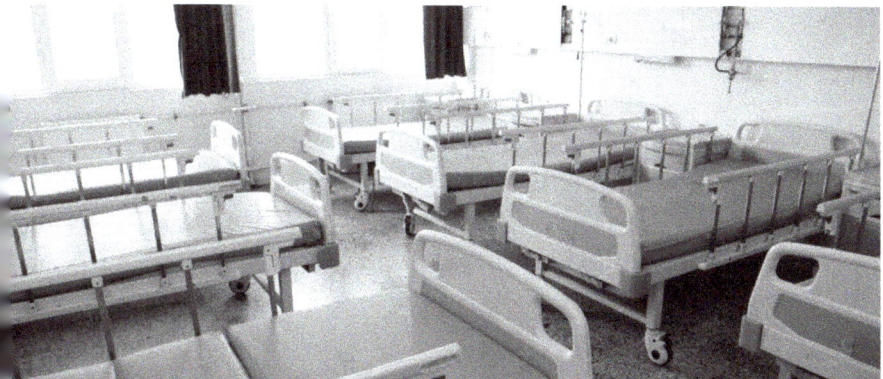

Solving the Empty Bed Problem Is Not as Simple as Throwing Out Mattresses

The effort to reduce the overall number of hospital beds to maximize available use as a way of bringing down costs was rejected by hospital administrators because beds were built in specialized wards, specific to types of care that patients could receive at any given moment.

As one New England hospital chief executive explained,

"Officially we have 90 percent occupancy at the moment and that is what we run most of the year. Do we get rid of the 10 percent extra beds? No, they aren't extra because you can't put a person with a fracture in the psych ward or an ulcer in the OB section. We have 51 empty beds and only three of them could – should – be used for someone with a 'normal' illness."

(Quoted in Barocci 1981, p. 32)

The ironic consequence of an excess of hospital beds, as assessed in the 1970s, was the decision to eliminate them by closing whole hospitals rather than trim excess in large hospitals.

One Way to Control Costs is to Fix Costs

CODE	DESCRIPTION
CRITICAL CARE	
99291	Critical care, minutes
99292	Critical care
PROCEDURES	
62270	Spinal punc
62272	Spinal punc
62273	Injection
31500	Intubation
93503	Insertion
92950	Cardiopul
ADVANCE CARE PLANNING	
99497	Advance ca forms (with professional
99498	Advance ca procedure
PROLONGED SERVICE	
99356	Prolonged service; first
99357	Prolonged addition to
TELEMEDICINE	
0188T	Remote critically ill
0189T	Remote in addition to
G0508	Telehealth the patient
G0509	Telehealth with the pat
INTERPROFESSIONAL	
99446	Interprofes physician qualified he
99447	Interprofes physician, 11
99448	Interprofes physician, 21
99449	Interprofes physician, 3

As part of the long-term effort to standardize hospital practices and physician decision-making – and to slow the growth of Medicare spending – the federal government introduced **Diagnostic Related Groups** (DRGs) in the 1980s. These led to the creation of now-pervasive billing codes.

With DRGs, hospitals are paid a fixed amount based on the diagnosis of the patient rather than the specific services provided. This system was intended to incentivize hospitals to deliver care more efficiently since they would retain any unspent funds but would have to absorb any costs beyond the DRG payment.

Did it work? The introduction of DRGs led to a reduction in the average length of hospital stays and slowed the growth rate of hospital spending for a period. "This kind of hospital screen is proving effective in the experience of an increasing number of corporations and in Medicare demonstrations," wrote former US Secretary of Health, Education, and Welfare Joseph Califano. (Califano 1986, p. 205)

However, no sooner had the program been implemented when it became apparent that the system could be gamed. As early as 1981, when prototype DRG systems were being tested, Donald Simborg, MD, Chief Medical Information Officer at the University of California, San Francisco (UCSF), observed the potential for what he called "DRG Creep" – reporting a more expensive diagnosis (or multiple diagnoses) in order for a hospital to receive higher payments. (Simborg 1981)

Turns Out, Hospitals Are Not Factories

Why It Matters

Mechanisms of mass production that work for conventional factories, such as standardization of parts, routinization of process, and shaping customers' interests, have often failed to work in complex healthcare systems, preventing the achievement of efficiencies to control costs.

Providing care is impossible to routinize completely. It is resistant to automation, despite computer-aided diagnostics and AI. Unable to choreograph workers' movements precisely, management had to enforce discipline at the level of scheduling, using time as a mechanism of control, though this is often disregarded owing to heavy demands.

The analogy of hospitals to factories was based on an ideal of scientific objectivity, specialization, and resource management, but healthcare has proved resistant to producing predictable outcomes.

In short, the **human element** is central in hospitals, not just in terms of patient care but also in the form of interactions among medical professionals, patients, and their families. Emotional, psychological, and social factors play a significant role in healthcare delivery.

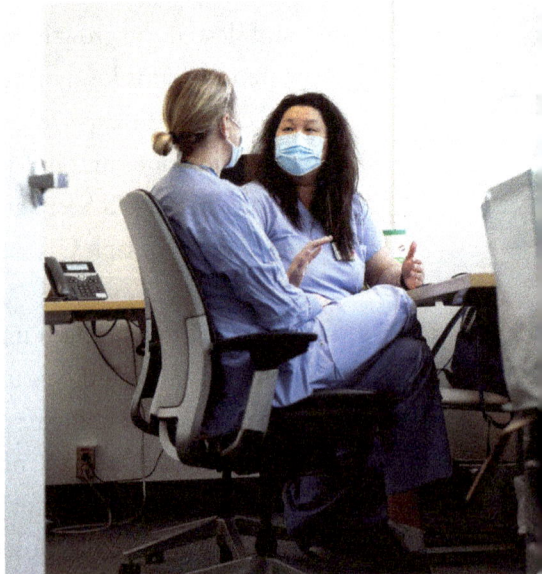

SUMMARY OF MAIN POINTS

Numerous efforts attempted **to control the rising costs** of hospital care. Here are five key measures taken by the government, insurance industry, and hospital groups:

1. The implementation of Medicare and Medicaid marked the beginning of federal involvement to control hospital reimbursement rates. Initially, payments were based on hospital charges, but as we saw this led to increased costs. Over time, the government began negotiating and capping reimbursement rates to better control spending.

2. The establishment of Diagnostic Related Groups (DRGs) in 1983 under the Medicare Prospective Payment System (PPS) categorized hospital cases into specific groups with fixed payment amount based on the type of treatment and diagnosis. The DRG system incentivized hospitals to reduce unnecessary services and improve efficiency, as payments were no longer based on the volume of services provided but on predetermined rates.

3. Certificate of Need (CON) Programs originated in the 1960s and expanded through the 1970s and were implemented by many states under the encouragement of federal law. These programs required hospitals and healthcare providers to obtain state approval before expanding facilities or services. The goal was to control the construction of new facilities and avoid redundant services, which could drive up healthcare costs through competition that did not necessarily improve quality or outcomes.

4. The Health Maintenance Organization Act of 1973 encouraged the development of HMOs, which were designed to provide coordinated, preventive care while controlling costs through capitation—paying a fixed fee per patient. These organizations limited unnecessary hospital stays and procedures by emphasizing preventive care and requiring primary care physician referrals for specialized services.

5. The Balanced Budget Act of 1997 act expanded the use of the DRG payment system and incorporated measures such as the reduction of payment updates and caps on cost-based reimbursements for outpatient services.

But increases in hospital costs continued to be driven by:

1. Population growth and longer life expectancy, projecting increased hospital utilization.

2. An oversupply of hospital beds, following aggressive hospital construction, created a need to induce demand for those beds.

3. Expansion of health insurance through Medicare and Medicaid covering hospital care.

4. The shift in physicians care to treat patients in hospitals rather than their own offices to use centralized resources.

5. The introduction of more elaborate and extensive diagnostic testing and laboratory services.

4

Insurers

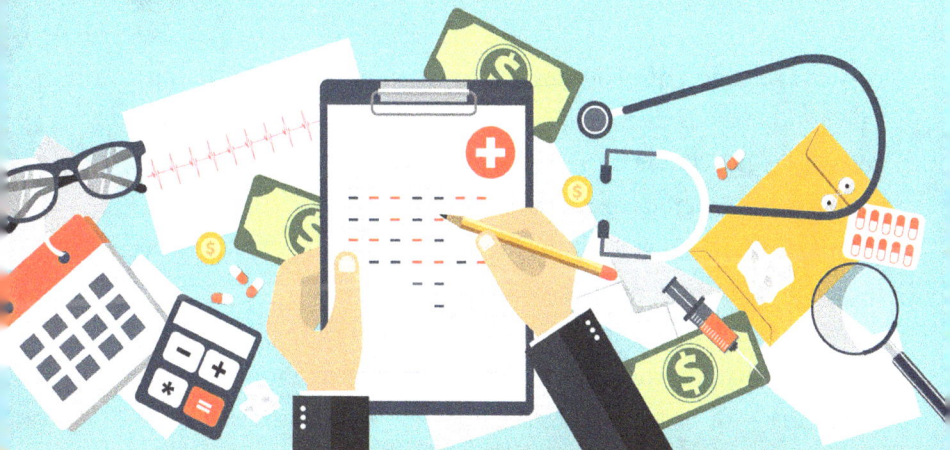

Five Factors That Link Healtl

1.

Moral hazard. A popular theory among economists, the idea is that insured individuals use services more when the majority of the bill is paid by insurers. The moral hazard refers to the consequences of overutilization that then drives up insurance costs, prohibiting lower-income consumers from purchasing insurance (resulting in a "welfare loss"). (Arrow 1963/2001; Pauly 1968)

2.

Physician-induced demand. This is based on the fact that physicians are responsible for most decisions that involve spending. Under fee-for-service reimbursement policies, more services are prone to be ordered, ultimately raising insurance rates or (in the case of Medicare and Medicaid) the burden on taxpayers. (Rice 1983)

3.

Adverse selection of plans among consumers. The notion here is that, in an open market where consumers can choose insurance plans, the sick choose more generous plans. When sick and healthy people enroll in different plans, those plans with a higher proportion of poor risks charge more than if they insured an average mix of people. This results in high premiums that discourage healthy consumers from choosing such plans with better coverage. (Cutler and Zeckhauser 2000)

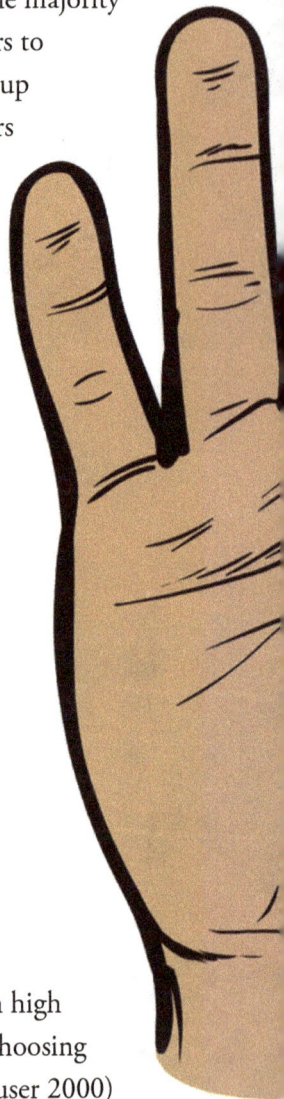

Care Costs to Insurance

4.

Administrative costs. Insurance administration is a primary driver of increased national healthcare expenditures, which (when coupled with accounting and clinical administrative costs) account for up to 25 percent of national health expenditures. (Chernew and Mintz 2021) Private insurers cited higher costs of processing Medicare and Medicaid claims as the cause of higher healthcare expenditures in the last twenty years. (Himmelstein et al. 2020)

5.

Market consolidation. As hospitals and providers consolidate to have better negotiating power with insurance companies, it can reduce competition in the market. This can drive up prices, as larger health systems with more market share can command better reimbursement from insurers. (MedPac 2020) Consolidation in the private health insurance industry also leads to premium increases. (Dafny 2015)

According to Blue Cross / Blue Shield, healthcare is costly because of three "key factors": the cost of prescription drugs, the drawn-out expense of managing chronic disease, and Americans' unhealthy lifestyles.

BlueCross BlueShield

The Health of America ›   CONTACT US

Member Services   Find a Doctor   Individuals & Families   Employers   Medicare   About Us   Learn

Why does healthcare cost so much?

Three Key Factors Driving U.S. Healthcare Costs

PRESCRIPTION DRUGS

etween 2010 and 2025, prescription drug prices are expected to increase by 136 percent.

CHRONIC DISEASES

Treating chronic diseases accounts for 86 percent of U.S. healthcare costs.

LIFESTYLE

Americans' unhealthy lifestyle choices are li chronic conditions.

wth in U.S. Prescription Drug Spending

icription drugs play a critical role in helping prevent, nage and cure various conditions and diseases, yet the ts are straining the budgets of families, businesses taxpayers alike.

The High Cost of Treating Chronic Diseases

Chronic diseases and conditions—such as arthritis, obesity, cancer and heart disease—are among the most common, costly and often preventable of all health problems.

How We Live Affects Healthcare Cos

Read how BCBS companies are enabling he and improving healthcare quality and afford

VIEW INF

https://www.bcbs.com/issues-indepth/why-does-healthcare-cost-so-much
Accessed June 2023

However, from a non-insurance industry point of view, health insurers also have a role to play in making care costly.

> *Prior to the 1930s there was virtually no health insurance in the United States. Americans personally paid more than 90 percent of their hospital and doctors' bills. What coverage existed aimed at replacing some part of the wages lost due to illness or accident."*
>
> (Califano 1986, p. 40)

In nineteenth-century America, shopping for healthcare was financially straightforward. Buying medicine (whether herbal or "patented" nostrums) was akin to buying food; staying at a hospital was akin to a hotel stay. Payment to doctors was negotiated. As Sue Lowden, the former Chair of the Nevada Republican Party, famously pointed out, "You know, before we all started having healthcare, in the olden days, our grandparents, they would bring a chicken to the doctor." (Adams 2010)

But by the 1920s, health insurance plans began to emerge, first as incentives to stay with an employer, then as a government plan to offset the expense of healthcare for vulnerable populations, then in the later twentieth century as a for-profit industry.

In 1940, about 12 million Americans had health insurance coverage. By 1960, over 122 million were enrolled in private health insurance plans. (Thomasson 2002, p. 234) As of 2021, over 300 million (above 90% of the US population) have health insurance. (US Census Bureau)

A Short History of Health Insurance Part I: The First Failure of US National Health Insurance

Most industrial societies consider the health of the working class a primary concern, ensuring productivity that is essential for the economic growth of the nation. Workmen's compensation plans, which protected workers from economic loss resulting from a work-related event, were predecessors to plans that provided health insurance for other vulnerable populations: those in old age, the disabled, dependents, and children.

In the US during the 1910s, organizations such as the American Association for Labor Legislation (organized in 1906, whose members included President Woodrow Wilson) spearheaded campaigns to introduce "social insurance" on a state-by-state basis. In 1915, these efforts were supported by a group of physicians who created a "Social Insurance Committee" within the American Medical Association (AMA). (Numbers 1978)

Although by 1920 forty-three states had enacted workmen's compensation plans, the course of World War I changed the national narrative about further health insurance legislation. By this time, the AMA had decisively dropped its support for social insurance.

Immediately following World War I, discussion of "government control" of healthcare (or anything) began to sound like dictatorship, and a propaganda campaign (funded by the AMA) condemned such efforts as *socialist* political ideology that America had just fought a war against. (Dolan 2016)

This established a long-standing narrative that government-run health insurance programs were un-American, creating a favorable environment for private healthcare enterprise.

Doctors Initially Supported Government Insurance

Why? It was a way of ensuring they were paid.

In the 1910s, the leadership of the AMA was broadly supportive of the government providing insurance to assist in paying for medical care, recognizing that it was becoming more difficult for individuals to afford care. The costs of healthcare in the early twentieth century were increasingly beyond reach for a number of reasons, including:

- Advances in medical technology, surgical techniques, and pharmaceuticals. As medical knowledge and capabilities grew, so did the costs associated with new treatments, equipment, and medications.

- Urbanization and hospital growth. With growing populations and an increase in the use of advanced medical technologies, care shifted from small clinics and into centralized hospitals with high capital, labor, and operational costs.

"The American Medical Association declares its opposition to the institution of any plan embodying the system of compulsory contributory insurance against illness, or any other plan of compulsory insurance which provides for medical service to be rendered [to] contributors or their dependents, provided, controlled, or regulated by any state or Federal government."

(American Medical Association 1920)

But After WWII, Doctors Were Against It

While government insurance plans might offer vulnerable populations financial assistance to obtain healthcare, studies of European plans, such as in Britain and France that were implemented in the 1940s, suggested that the government might exercise too much control over clinical practice, treatment options, and professional fees. (Quadagno 2006)

Why It Matters

The professional opposition to national healthcare insurance delayed the government for decades from doing what the profession feared: controlling ever-increasing prices of healthcare that might impact clinicians' income.

"It is a sad fact that through the 1930s and the early 1940s the American Medical Association did not believe in voluntary sickness insurance and did almost everything possible to prevent its development."   United Auto Workers President Walter Reuther to Congress, 1961

"These were sporadic money-making schemes devised by various entrepreneurs."   Dr. Edward Annis, former AMA President, 1961 (Quotes from Rayack 1967a, p. 3)

The AMA repeatedly discredited voluntary insurance, calling it a threat to the competitive position of physicians and claiming it would lead to loss of control over medical practice to government or commercial interests. As the Great Depression continued through the 1930s and popular interest in public insurance grew, the attacks against national health insurance were amplified. (Rayack 1967)

In essence, the economic concerns expressed by the AMA were:

• That government-controlled health insurance might lead to fixed fee schedules, potentially reducing professional income.

• That government bureaucracy would interfere with the practice of medicine, would make that practice more expensive, and would make reimbursement more cumbersome.

The Arrival of the Blues

Amidst growing interest in government-sponsored health insurance in the 1930s, the medical professions found it prudent to be proactive in addressing concerns about costs and devised plans that allowed physicians to retain a considerable amount of control over their own business model, fees, and the medical services they provided.

Following a successful experiment of a group hospital prepayment plan at Baylor University (for a payment of 50 cents a month the hospital provided complete hospital care when needed), the American Hospital Association and the American College of Surgeons backed the expansion of prepaid group hospitalization (with participating hospitals identified with a Blue Cross symbol). However, professional tensions arose in the debate over whether physicians' fees would be covered under these plans (or just hospital costs).

In 1939, the California Physicians Service started a corollary program called Blue Shield, which was the first service prepayment plan for physicians, with 5,000 doctors participating within the first five months. In the 1940s, the United Auto Workers secured health benefits for its members, prompting the major auto companies, along with other industry powers, to offer Blue Cross and Blue Shield (BCBS) insurance. The insurers quickly enrolled millions of members. (Cunningham and Cunningham 1997)

All along, the Blues (referring to both Cross and Shield) enjoyed a tax-exempt status as nonprofit organizations. (Eilers 1961) However, the Tax Reform Act of 1986 altered the tax status for Blue Cross Blue Shield plans. In order to maintain their tax-exempt status, BCBS plans were required to meet certain criteria, including spending at least 60% of their premium revenues on healthcare services.

Over time, many BCBS plans shifted from nonprofit to for-profit status, succumbing to the competitive pressures in the health insurance market.

With post-World War II efforts to control inflation and ever-rising healthcare costs that created barriers to care for disadvantaged and older Americans, the federal government again pushed for national insurance, prompting professional medical organizations to strengthen their support and coordination of the Blues.

The Bottom Line

By backing private insurance plans of its own design, the medical profession kept at bay nationalized control over healthcare costs, creating an environment that allowed costs to escalate. In short, the blockade of "social health insurance" made healthcare more costly.

A Short History of Health Insurance Part II: The Role of Employers

In 1942, President Roosevelt established the National War Labor Board (similar to the Board established during WWI in 1918) to arbitrate labor disputes and prevent strikes that might impact the war effort. That same year, the United Steelworkers of America (USWA) union was established and quickly became a powerful force when it joined the Congress of Industrial Organizations (CIO).

As part of the effort to control inflation, the National War Labor Board restricted how much employers could increase salaries to attract or retain workers in a highly competitive market owing to war mobilization. However, in 1943 the Board, facing a confrontation with the CIO, allowed **wages to be supplemented with fringe benefits**.

This created employer-sponsored health insurance programs. That same year, the Internal Revenue Service determined that employer contributions to health insurance premiums were exempt from employees' income tax, making the benefit an attractive addition to employment packages and an important lever for future union negotiations.

Post-war inflation pushed industrial labor unions again to bargain collectively for cost-of-living increases. The steel industry pushed back.

As a result, the USWA organized strikes in the steel industry in 1946, 1949, 1952, 1956, and 1959, each time demanding not only higher wages but health benefits (and other fringe benefits) as a condition of employment. (Winant 2021)

In the 1950s, many Western industrialized countries nationalized their health insurance, ensuring the provision of care to all citizens. But in the US, **the 1954 Internal Revenue Code revision solidified the tax advantages of employer-sponsored health insurance** by making company contributions to employee benefit plans tax deductible. Instead of the government organizing healthcare, the US shifted that responsibility to employers. (Coombs 2005)

The end of the 116-day USWA strike in 1959 involved requiring steel companies to pay the entire premium for health insurance, which set a new standard across major American industries. In 1961, General Motors, Ford, and Chrysler accepted similar healthcare schemes in their negotiations with the United Automobile Workers. Throughout the 1960s and 1970s, business and labor kept expanding health insurance coverage and benefits, reducing consumer incentives to "shop around" and removing physician incentives to hold down fees and utilization.

Meanwhile, the costs kept growing. "American businesses spent about $90 billion in health insurance premiums in 1984, 38 percent of their 1984 pretax profits, more than they paid in dividends to their shareholders." (Califano 1986, p. 31)

I want to shop for private health insurance. I want to explore my options, you know, ask them: What can you do that's better than the other companies? It'll make them work harder for my business and they'll give me a better price.

As they say, the market enhances efficiency and improves consumer choice!

Been there, done that! But prices keep going up. Insurers say that prescription drugs and doctors' fees keep getting more expensive. Prices seem all over the place. I think if everyone banded together, as a single payer, then they would not have the ability to inflate prices. But I will admit this, it's better than me paying it all out of my own pocket!

Commercial Health Insurance Companies Enter the Market

Why It Matters

Despite conventional assumptions that the market will control costs when private companies compete for business, factors unique to the healthcare industry cause costs to increase. These include:

- High administrative costs related to navigating the complexity of regulations, billing, coding, and variable payment processes

- Limited bargaining power to negotiate prices with large-scale providers

- Biased benefit design that drives up prices disproportionately for certain segments of the population

- Market concentration that limits competitive pressure to lower costs and rewards the shareholders' profit motive

The success of Blue Cross and Blue Shield prodded commercial insurers to enter the health insurance market in the late 1930s and 1940s. Companies such as Metropolitan Life, Prudential, and Aetna, which had previously focused on life insurance or accident insurance, began offering health insurance products. These early commercial health insurance policies often provided coverage for both hospital and physician services and were structured more like indemnity plans.

The way commercial insurance companies underwrite policies and set premiums is varied and can lead to disparities in policy availability and costs.

Large for-profit, group insurance companies base their premiums on an "experience rating," charging sick people more than healthy individuals (rather than charge the same premium to all in a community). This provided opportunities to offer less expensive plans to segments of the population (employed, healthy, younger people) and grow their membership. But premiums were also based on race, lifestyle choices, the density of the serviced population, and the supply of physicians and hospitals in the area, leading to discrimination against communities of color and rural populations. (Thomasson 2002)

→ **These variable policies mean that some people pay higher healthcare costs than others**, though in 2014 the Affordable Care Act limited the factors that can be used to charge consumers greater health insurance premiums. (45 CFR Part 147)

While insurance coverage can foster an illusion that healthcare is not costly, the insurance industry bears the impact of increased costs. When the industry hurts, it hits the pockets of policy holders.

Administrative Costs Keep Growing Within a Complex Industry

Why It Matters

The complexity of insurance billing, coding, and payment terms across multiple platforms helps create inefficiencies. This complexity makes it challenging for consumers to shop for the best prices or to understand their financial responsibilities, leading to higher costs and unexpected bills.

→   Americans love choices. But providing options for physicians, clinics, or services makes billing more complicated and regulatory compliance more onerous. These costs may be hidden from patients seeking care given the opacity of industry negotiations.

→   Negotiations between other healthcare sectors, such as pharmaceutical companies and medical device firms, are complex. There is little coordinated cost containment when it comes to pricing drugs or technologies, resulting in a high administrative burden when seeking alternatives, negotiating rebates, or studying effective utilization practices. (Chernew and Mintz 2021)

Insurers Are Stuck In The Middle

A number of organizations competing against each other have limited bargaining power.

Insurers (excepting HMOs) are intermediaries between providers and patients. They negotiate with healthcare organizations, the pharmaceutical industry, technology firms, and (increasingly) the government on the price of goods and services that they will cover for their policy holders.

To remedy this, insurers can threaten to ban their policy holders from seeking care with those providers, or not cover the use of certain products. But by doing so, the insurer runs the risk of upsetting its customers who, in the US, have historically demanded freedom of choice.

When the insurance industry pays higher reimbursements to healthcare providers, it raises premiums. Customers either pay more, seek a new insurer, or abandon their coverage.

A Short History of Health Insurance Part III: The Presence of Government Health Insurance

The long opposition to government-organized healthcare finance assistance came from multiple sources: organized medicine, powerful labor unions who saw it as a threat to union-sponsored insurance programs, insurance industry leaders who wanted to maintain market opportunities, and politicians whose anti-"socialist" rhetoric and criticism of "big government" appealed to some voters.

But after massive victories by Democrats in the 1964 elections, the decades-long effort to use the federal budget to provide "hospital insurance for the aged" moved closer to reality, and President Johnson was blunt in his commitment.

"I'll spend the goddamn money. I may cut back on some tanks. But not on health." President Lyndon Johnson to Congressman Wilbur Mills, 1965   (Dolan 2016, p. 21)

Medicare and Medicaid only passed through Congress after a compromise with Republican and right-of-center Democratic politicians.

In drafting and debating amendments to the Social Security Act (where Medicare laws were embedded), and in an effort to prevent their derailment through non-participation or physician strikes, **lawmakers spelled out the limits of the government's powers to interfere with providing healthcare**. One of the first paragraphs of the Medicare Act (1965), Section 1801, is titled "Prohibition Against Any Federal Interference," and states that:

> Nothing in this title shall be construed to authorize any Federal officer or employee to exercise any supervision or control over the practice of medicine or the manner in which medical services are provided, or over the selection, tenure, or compensation of any officer or employee of any institution, agency, or person providing health services; or to exercise any supervision or control over the administration or operation of any such institution, agency, or person. (Dolan and Beitler 2022, p. 480)

While this part of the bill was written to mollify concerns that the government would control medical decision making to keep costs down, the consequence of the government's concession of regulatory power created a structural weakness in the administration of Medicare and Medicaid that has allowed the system to be manipulated and abused over a half century, leading to increased costs.

When Money Is No Barrier, Costs Go Up

"Approximately half of the total increase in medical expenditures during the 1960s was the result of increased utilization of medical services and not price inflation."

(Eisenberg and Rosoff 1978, p. 76)

Overutilization is a problem that emerged in the late 1960s after the passage of Medicare. When the government started funding healthcare for large segments of the population, hospitals and physicians suddenly took extraordinary interest in every aspect of their patients' health.

For decades, growth in Medicare payment to physicians far outstripped the growth in the economy as a whole. "From 1975 to 1983, Medicare Part B costs increased three times faster than the gross national product." (Geiger and Krol 1991, p. 244)

Medicare Part B reimbursed physicians for their services based on "customary-prevailing-reasonable" fees for their area. What determines *customary* fees for service provoked much debate, as did the explanations for why healthcare utilization increased throughout these years: Was it induced demand by physicians? Or patients demanding more care?

Keyword: "Moral Hazard"

A classic concept from the seminal work of Kenneth Aarow (1963) describing the change in people's behavior when they have insurance. When patients pay less for medical care, they utilize more of it. A RAND study on the "National Health Insurance Experiment" found that copays helped mitigate against excessive moral hazard utilization without eroding quality. (Brook et al. 2006; Finkelstein 2015)

Whether Public or Private, Certain Factors Elude Cost Control

➤ **Self-Regulated Fee Structures or Prevailing Market Customs Do Not Bring Down Costs**

For the medical profession to drop its objections to Medicare and Medicaid, the government agreed to reimburse on a fee-for-service model at a "reasonable" rate. What was considered reasonable was based on prevailing market conditions in a certain area. But each year, these fees, coupled with increasing use of medical services, sent the overall costs skyrocketing. The introduction of Professional Standards Review Organizations (PSROs) in the 1970s to monitor utilization and costs was a form of professional peer-review and did little to control costs. (Dolan and Beitler 2022)

➤ **Coverage for Chronic Diseases Escalates Costs**

The growing need to manage chronic diseases contributes substantially to more spending on health insurance. For example, a range of conditions linked to obesity, including diabetes, heart disease, hyperlipidemia, etc., are more widespread in the population, generating higher healthcare spending per capita. (Thorpe et al. 2005)

➤ **55% of Total Hospital Costs Go To Wages**

Higher costs go into a labor-intensive industry where wage increases are driven by labor shortages. (Lopez et al. 2020)

The Largest Payer (the Government) Has Historically Barred Itself From Negotiating Prices

Since the passage of Medicare and Medicaid, the government has introduced a number of reimbursement models and rates to determine fair pricing.

In 1983, the government introduced a Prospective Payment System (PPS), which provided specific reimbursement for services defined as necessary in a specific Diagnostic Related Group (DRG).

Policies set by the Affordable Care Act (2010) provided annual adjustments to Medicare payments to hospitals for productivity increases. While this has resulted in more efficient cost control measures than individually negotiating with providers according to prevailing market conditions (as private insurers do), certain healthcare costs, such as payment for prescription drugs under Medicare Part D, have not been subject to negotiation due to "non-interference" clauses in the legislation. However, the Inflation Reduction Act of 2022 allows the Centers for Medicare and Medicaid Services (CMS) to engage in price negotiations for a number of costly medications, though this is being challenged in court by the drug industry. (Luhby 2023)

The Bottom Line

Even though the government is the largest payer for healthcare services and could exercise considerable control over costs, many of the tactics used in collective bargaining are relinquished to conventional market forces or delegated to private insurance companies.

Case Study: Regulating Price Hikes

The tension between healthcare providers and insurers can be described as a war of attrition. In most cases, when physician groups or the drug industry insist on charging more for services and products, insurers will concede and in turn raise their rates for policy holders. However, when the state or federal government prohibits insurers from raising premiums (for example, capping it at Medicare price index + 1 percent), then providers know that insurers' hands are tied, and prices do not increase at the same rate as in unregulated areas. (Baum et al. 2019)

Whether through major federal health reforms or targeted regulations, the government can have both direct and indirect effects on the cost of healthcare. Depending on the specific goal of the regulation, costs might increase, decrease, or remain relatively unchanged.

In short, government intervention through regulations can impact insurance industry behavior and yield cost controls.

In Summary

The US health insurance industry, like other sectors of healthcare, has pursued open market solutions to control costs, to create efficiencies, and to deliver profit to its investors.

However, it has failed on the first two counts because healthcare is distinctively complex and unpredictable.

The many factors that affect population health, the lack of knowledge among consumers on what they are buying, and the varied regulatory environment across fifty states, do not fit conventional market models.

For insurance companies to provide the financial assistance necessary for individuals to access healthcare (which is the function of their policies), it consistently has been necessary to increase costs.

5

Pharmaceuticals

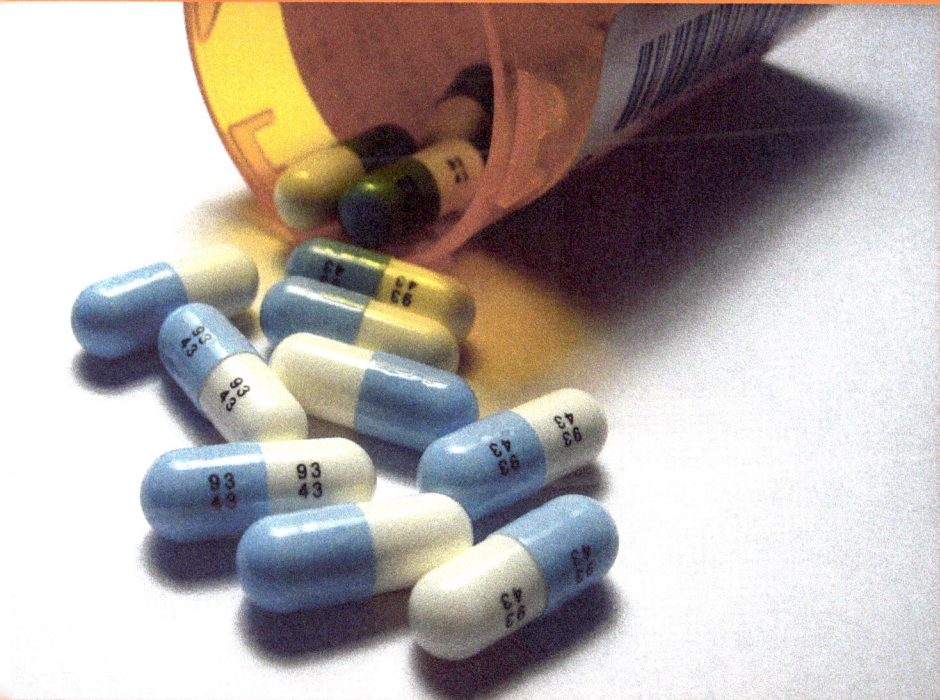

At first glance, the role of pharmaceutical companies in driving up healthcare costs is plain: they charge a lot for their products and sell a lot of products. But unpeel some layers and different explanations emerge for the pricing of drugs and how the demand for them is fueled by marketing strategies that encourage the perception of need.

Why It Matters

Americans spend several times what people in other developed countries do for the same brand-name drugs. (Rosenthal 2023) Why are medicines so expensive? High prices result from the pharmaceutical industry's control of decisive scientific, legislative, and regulatory processes. The industry works hard to create demand for their products through aggressive advertising.

By The Numbers

According to data from the Centers for Medicare and Medicaid Services (CMS) and the US Bureau of Economic Analysis, prescription drug spending is one of the largest sectors of the Gross Domestic Product, ranked close to the categories of hospital care and physician services.

- In 2021, healthcare spending in the US grew 2.7% to $4.3 trillion, or $12,914 per person.
- This amounted to 18.3% of Gross Domestic Product (GDP). (Abramson 2022)
- Prescription drug spending in 2021 rose 7.8% to $378.0 billion, faster than 2020s 3.7% growth. As of April 2023, prescription drugs accounted for between 10-15% of total healthcare spending in the US.

tal U.S. Retail Drug Spending by Therapeutic Class, 2009 and 2019

ons of 2019 dollars

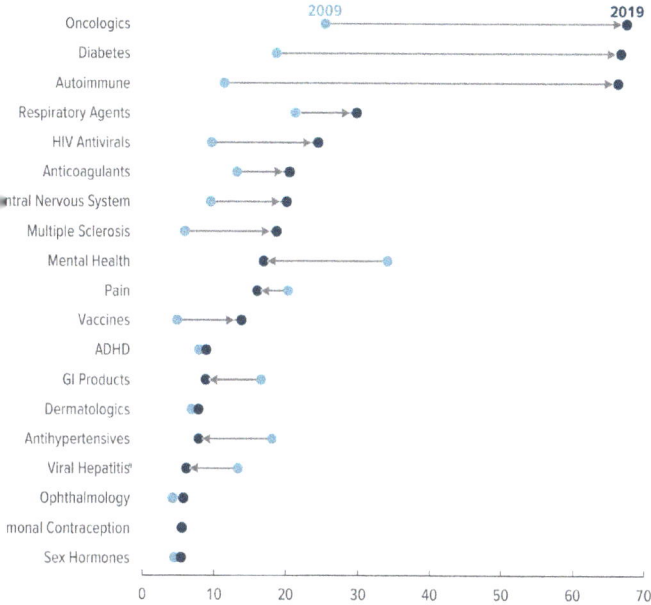

New drugs can lead to large increases in retail spending because they have higher prices, they are in high demand, or both. Spending decreases can result when patent protection expires on leading drugs and low-cost generic versions are introduced.

source: Congressional Budget Office, using data from IQVIA Institute for Human Data Science, *Medicine Spending and Affordability in the United States: *erstanding Patients' Costs for Medicines* (August 2020), Exhibit 24, https://tinyurl.com/5655tnoc; IMS Institute for Healthcare Informatics, *Medicines Use Spending Shifts: A Review of the Use of Medicines in the U.S. in 2014* (April 2015), p. 40, https://tinyurl.com/3bk9oufn, and *Medicine Use and Shifting ts of Healthcare: A Review of the Use of Medicines in the United States in 2013* (April 2014), Appendix 8, https://go.usa.gov/xsaFR. See www.cbo.gov/ lication/57025#data.

Various Pharmaceutical Spending as a Share of Net Sales, 2000 vs 2018

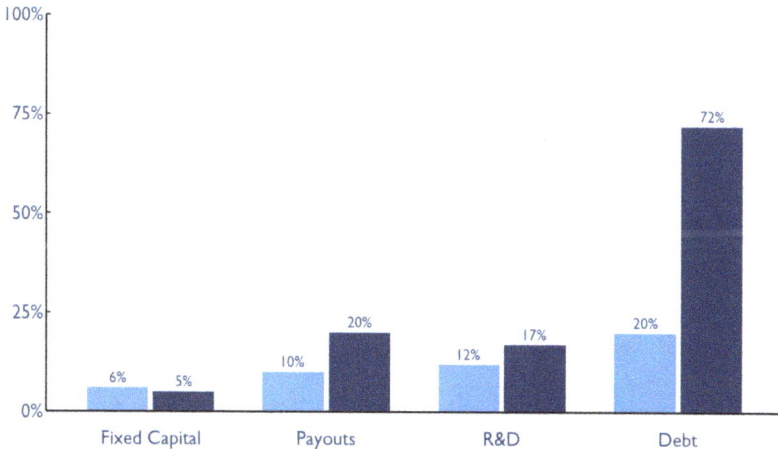

Source: SOMO

The Big Picture

Since 1945, several industry forces have driven price growth. These include the development of employer-provider-insurer healthcare delivery networks; increasing industry management of clinical trials; greater ability to influence clinicians' understanding of prescription drugs via direct-to-consumer (DTC) advertising and Continuing Medical Education (CME) subsidies; a growing role in affecting federal and state laws; and, after World War II, the inclusion of global patent protection for US companies in international trade agreements.

The pharmaceutical industry epitomized the financialization of American corporations and the rise of the shareholder. Eighteen pharmaceutical companies were among the 466 Standard & Poor's 500 companies that were publicly listed between 2009 and 2018. During these years, these companies had combined profits of $588 billion. At the same time, they spent about $50 billion more than that on stock buybacks and dividends, rewarding investors with higher-value shares by reducing the total number of outstanding shares. (Tulum and Lazonick 2018)

These numbers tell a story that goes beyond revenue, costs, and profits. Pharmaceutical therapies achieved unprecedented clinical and social status as manufacturers portrayed their products as examples of cutting-edge science.

The Trinity Creating Costly Drugs

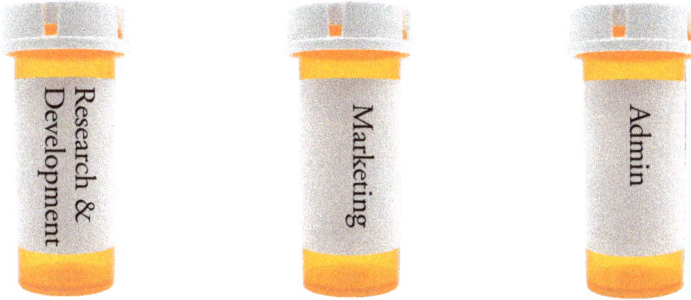

Research and Development (R&D): One widely cited study by the Tufts Center for the Study of Drug Development estimated the cost to be around $2.6 billion per new drug (DiMasi 2016), in part because only about 10 percent of drugs in clinical trials make it to market, though costs vary across drug candidates. (PhRMA data sheet, CBO April 2021, p. 2)

Marketing: A 2019 study found that, from 1997 through 2016, "spending on medical marketing of drugs, disease awareness campaigns, health services, and laboratory testing increased from $17.7 to 29.9 billion." The fastest growth was in direct-to-consumer (DTC) advertising. (Schwartz and Woloshin, 2019)

Legal and Administrative Costs: Pharmaceutical companies allocate large sums for (a) managing clinical trials; (b) satisfying governmental regulatory requirements; and (c) servicing litigation fees and settlements.

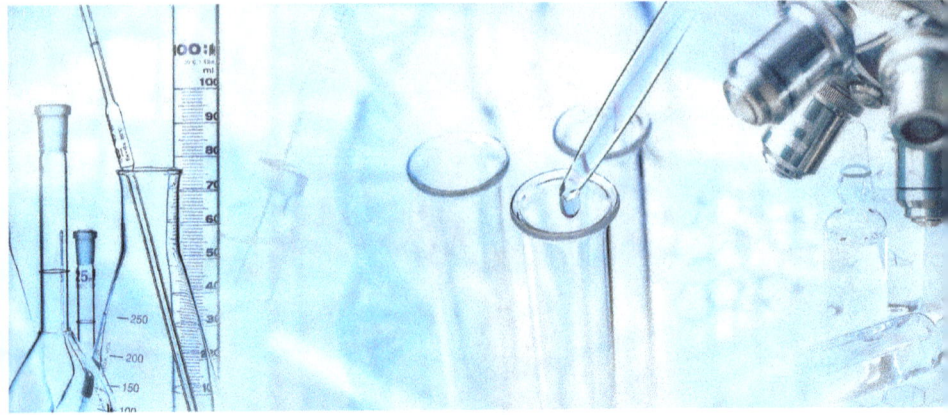

Research and Development

For decades, the pharmaceutical industry has cited R&D costs – which it claims average more than $2 billion per drug – as a major price driver. But is that fully accurate?

A 2020 study used publicly available data on 63 of the 355 drugs and biologic agents that the FDA approved between 2009 and 2018. The estimated median R&D cost per product was $1.1 billion, which included costs of failed trials. (Wouters et al. 2020)

Calculating R&D spending is complex. Private companies regard such costs as confidential business information and lack standardized reporting requirements. Add to that the length of time it takes for such research to occur, along with overlapping and indirect costs associated with multiple projects, and exact numbers are hard to derive. Such uncertainty and opacity in drug development expenses help to obscure the impact that R&D has on the cost of prescription drugs.

High R&D Costs = High Drug Costs: Debunking a Popular Myth?

While touted as a major expense that must be recovered, a report by the Congressional Budget Office stated that: "A drug's sunk R&D costs – that is, the costs already incurred in developing that drug – do not influence its price."

Instead, the price of a new prescription drug is calculated on market forces (payers' willingness to pay) and how to maximize future profits after manufacturing and distribution costs. Therefore, the way the market itself is perceived to bear the cost of a new drug, and the company's desire to maximize profits, contribute to the rising cost of healthcare.

ECONOMIC POLICY

How an $84,000 drug got its price: 'Let's hold our position ... whatever the headlines'

By Carolyn Y. Johnson and Brady Dennis
December 1, 2015 at 2:27 p.m. EST

The Washington Post

"Prices have become the prize"

Gilead's Solvadi, a hepatitis C drug that gained federal approval in 2013, was priced at $84,000 for a twelve-week course of treatment. Defending its price point as "in line with previous standards of care" and the fact that the company had assistance programs for uninsured patients, the cost was set with an eye to maximizing shareholder return while not breaking the tolerance threshold for insured patients. (Johnson and Dennis 2015) Too steep? Bach (2014) argued that the pharmaceutical industry has insufficient incentive to invest in novel therapies because the "first entrant" to the marketplace will not be compensated for innovating a new class of drugs, necessitating the reward of high sales prices.

Patents Encourage Innovation but Exclude Competition

If a company expends huge sums of money developing a drug that may help treat a disease, and then engages in a multi-year clinical trial to prove its safety and efficacy, shouldn't it be rewarded with the right to sell it without interference by competitors who copy the results? Patents provide protection. And because it is recognized that safety regulations require lengthy periods of testing of new drugs, pharmaceutical companies are given a seven-year period of exclusive marketing rights to sell.

A company that develops a new therapeutic drug can maximize its profit potential by capturing market exclusivity through patents or through government protection under the Orphan Drug Act (enacted in 1983) that encouraged development of drugs to treat conditions affecting fewer than 200,000 people. (Yin 2023)

Yet patents create monopolies that allow companies to set high prices. If competition in the market does not check this, what does? Either government regulations that limit pricing, or consumers organizing to demand lower costs. In theory, at least, insurers could decide not to pay.

When patents expire, should other companies need to go through the same lengthy clinical trial testing of their version of the product, thus delaying or discouraging the arrival of generic alternatives that could lower the cost to consumers? The Hatch-Waxman Act answered no, and paved the way for faster entry of generic drugs.

Generics

While the Hatch-Waxman Act of 1984 extended patent protection to drug developers to account for five years of clinical trials; it also created a pathway for the faster arrival of alternatives when patents expire, by allowing FDA approval of generics without clinical trials. (Congressional Budget Office 2021)

"For example, between 2012 and 2017, the United States spent $6.8 billion solely due to price increases on the existing brand name cancer drugs; in the same period, the rest of the world spent $1.7 billion *less* due to decreases in the prices of similar drugs." (Rajkumar 2020, p.4)

The Hatch-Waxman Act

The Drug Price Competition and Patent Term Restoration Act (Public Law 98-417) of 1984 addressed problems with existing patent laws that discouraged companies from pursuing innovations in healthcare and delayed generic alternatives that would help lower costs from entering the marketplace. The law has three main elements:

- Extending the term of pharmaceutical patents by up to five years in recognition that such protections should begin before FDA approves its entrance to the marketplace;
- Easing the path for generic manufacturers to gain FDA approval without repeating costly clinical trials required of the original innovators;
- Allowing companies to undertake a costly challenge to a patent (for being invalid or arguing they will not infringe) with a period of generic drug market exclusivity – a **regulatory exclusivity** that encourages development in areas such as orphan drugs (for a disorder that affects under 200,000 people in the US) or pediatric drugs.

*"The most important reason for the high cost of prescription drugs is the existence of monopoly."
(Rajkumar 2020)*

Keywords: Monopoly, Monopsony, Oligopoly

A **monopoly** refers to the exclusive right granted to the company to manufacture, use, and sell the patented drug for a certain period, typically 20 years from the date of filing. During this patent-protected period, the pharmaceutical company can exclude others from making, using, or selling the drug, which effectively allows the company to operate without competition for that specific medication, often leading to higher prices.

A **monopsony** is where a single buyer of goods and services controls the market. It can emerge when a seller has a monopoly (afforded through a patent, for example) which encourages a purchaser to grow large enough to create a countervailing market power. This is often accomplished by the government or insurance companies in the healthcare sector.

An **oligopoly** in pharmaceutical pricing refers to a structure where a few companies control the market for certain drugs. These dominant firms have significant market power to set prices above competitive levels. The lack of sufficient competition can diminish price wars and lead to higher costs for consumers. Collaboration or tacit understandings among these firms, whether legal or not, can also result in less aggressive pricing strategies and innovation, potentially impacting overall healthcare costs.

Marketing

There's no debate over whether pharmaceutical companies put a lot of money into marketing. But because the industry guards marketing data fiercely, reliable numbers are elusive.

Pharmaceutical companies spend heavily on marketing in order to create the belief among physicians and patients that new treatments are at the cutting edge of scientific advance. This is usually not true. (Petersen 2008, p. 46)

Informative or Manipulative?

Direct-to-consumer advertising begs the question of whether it is encouraging more educated decisions about purchasing a product or motivating consumers to overuse or try something unnecessary.

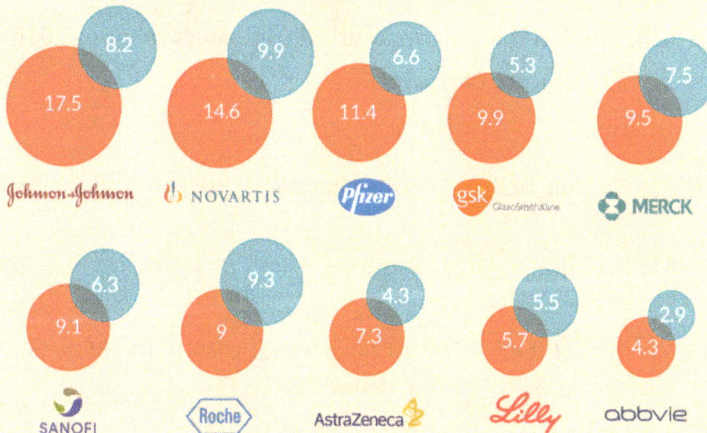

HOW MUCH DOES BIG PHARMA SPEND ON:
SALES & MARKETING vs. RESEARCH & DEVELOPMENT

Johnson&Johnson — 8.2 / 17.5
NOVARTIS — 9.9 / 14.6
Pfizer — 6.6 / 11.4
gsk GlaxoSmithKline — 5.3 / 9.9
MERCK — 7.5 / 9.5

SANOFI — 6.3 / 9.1
Roche — 9.3 / 9
AstraZeneca — 4.3 / 7.3
Lilly — 5.5 / 5.7
abbvie — 2.9 / 4.3

Credit: León Markovitz / Dadaviz / BBC

IN US $ BILLION, FOR 2013

Where Do the Billions of Marketing Dollars Go?

According to an analysis published in JAMA by Schwartz and Woloshin (2019), drug marketing increased from $17.7 billion in 1997 to $29.9 billion in 2016. During that same time, spending on direct-to-consumer (DTC) advertising increased from $2.1 billion to $9.6 billion.

Of the $20.3 billion that pharmaceutical companies spent in 2016 on marketing to healthcare professionals:

☞ $5.6 billion went to pharmaceutical salespeople and their support

☞ $13.5 billion for free samples

☞ $979 million for direct physician payments (e.g., speaking fees, meals) related to specific drugs

☞ $59 million for disease education

Is Marketing Money Well Spent?

❝ *The pharmaceutical industry spends approximately the same amount of money on marketing as it does on innovation investments." (Lakdawalla 2018)*

Pro: Marketing makes it more profitable to sell new products. Without the prospect of economic reward, innovation stagnates.

Con: Such behavior harms social welfare and is more likely to raise healthcare costs than contain them.

Gift Giving

In 2015, about one in every seven American physicians received opioid-related gifts from pharmaceutical companies; another analysis put the figure for family physicians at one in every five. (Hollander et al. 2020, Hadland et al. 2017, Marks 2020)

Lobbying

In the early 2000s, the industry employed two lobbyists for every member of Congress. (Petersen 2008, p. 10; Abramson 2022, p. 96)

Between 2006 and 2015, opioid companies alone spent $880 million on lobbying and campaign contributions. This compared with $4 million spent by groups advocating limits on opioid prescribing and was about eight times what the "gun lobby" spent on the same activities. (Center for Public Integrity 2016a, 2016b; Marks 2020) In 2018, individual pharmaceutical companies and their trade organization spent about $220 million on lobbying. (Rajkumar 2020, p. 2)

For decades, this effort has yielded strong results in patent protection, tax rules, and regulatory scrutiny (or its absence). The US Congress consistently has played a key role in policies that have helped create today's industry.

Pharmaceutical companies have poured hundreds of millions of dollars into continuing medical education (CME), required courses for licensure, which have become "a major focus for covert promotional activity." (Goldacre 2013, p. 264) (Rosenthal 2023)

One study found that corporations give non-profits charitable grants with the explicit goal of eliciting favorable comments during regulatory reviews. (Marks 2020, Bertrand et al. 2018, p. 1)

Bottom Line:
Lobbying efforts can result in policies that favor the industry's financial interests, which may not always align with the goal of reducing healthcare costs for consumers.

Legal and Administrative

Pharmaceutical companies incur significant legal and administrative costs as they develop, then extend and protect, their therapeutic franchises.

In 2010 the National Academy of Medicine said that the US spends about twice as much as it needs to on billing and insurance-related costs, or about $250 billion every year. (Gee and Spiro 2019)

FIGURE 1

Administrative costs comprise a larger share of health care spending in the United States than in other high-income countries

Administrative spending as a percentage of total health expenditures, 2016*

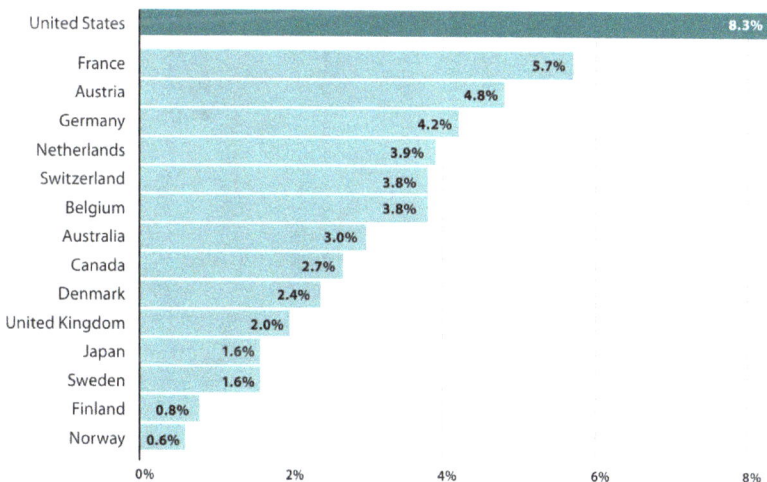

Country	Percentage
United States	8.3%
France	5.7%
Austria	4.8%
Germany	4.2%
Netherlands	3.9%
Switzerland	3.8%
Belgium	3.8%
Australia	3.0%
Canada	2.7%
Denmark	2.4%
United Kingdom	2.0%
Japan	1.6%
Sweden	1.6%
Finland	0.8%
Norway	0.6%

*Note: Data for Australia and Japan are for 2015; data for all other countries are for 2016.

Source: Organisation for Economic Co-operation and Development, "Health expenditure and financing," available at https://stats.oecd.org/index.aspx?DataSetCode=SHA (last accessed January 2019).

Making the Rules

Congress and the FDA have played major roles in creating today's pharmaceutical industry. Federal laws and regulations have defined commercial rights and requirements, created incentives, and given the industry overall favorable treatment in drug development, marketing, and finance.

1980

1983

1984

1988

1992

The Bayh-Dole Act enables small businesses and universities to control patent rights from government-sponsored research in their laboratories and to offer exclusive licenses to private firms.

The Hatch-Waxman Act extends patent protection to compensate for time spent by companies in premarket development. The length of the extension for a given drug was the sum of the time spent on FDA review before approval, plus half the time spent in clinical trials.

The Prescription Drug User Fee Act requires drug and biologics manufacturers to pay user fees for product applications and supplements; the fees are used only to speed up review and approval. The law requires the FDA to hire more reviewers and sets performance goals for the drug approval process.

The Orphan Drug Act's market exclusivity provision is attractive to manufacturers because the seven-year period starts from the date of FDA approval. Companies also receive substantial tax credits for some R&D spending on these drugs.

Congress enacts the Medicare Catastrophic Coverage Act, which includes limited prescription drug benefits and some cost-sharing for beneficiaries. The law is repealed about 18 months later, due to controversies over additional taxes and fees that elderly patients pay for coverage.

A full history through a federal lens would be vast, and it goes back much further than 1980. Here are key legislative and regulatory milestones that have shaped what Americans pay for prescription drugs today.

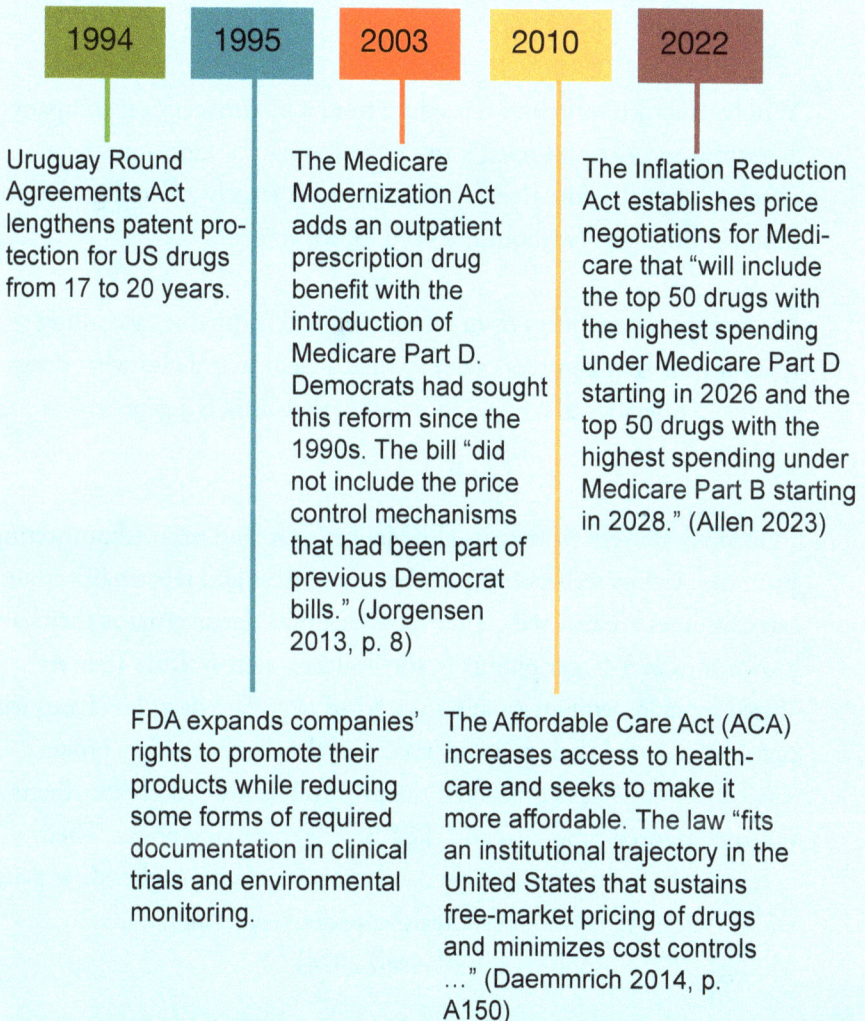

1994	1995	2003	2010	2022

1994 — Uruguay Round Agreements Act lengthens patent protection for US drugs from 17 to 20 years.

2003 — The Medicare Modernization Act adds an outpatient prescription drug benefit with the introduction of Medicare Part D. Democrats had sought this reform since the 1990s. The bill "did not include the price control mechanisms that had been part of previous Democrat bills." (Jorgensen 2013, p. 8)

2022 — The Inflation Reduction Act establishes price negotiations for Medicare that "will include the top 50 drugs with the highest spending under Medicare Part D starting in 2026 and the top 50 drugs with the highest spending under Medicare Part B starting in 2028." (Allen 2023)

1995 — FDA expands companies' rights to promote their products while reducing some forms of required documentation in clinical trials and environmental monitoring.

2010 — The Affordable Care Act (ACA) increases access to healthcare and seeks to make it more affordable. The law "fits an institutional trajectory in the United States that sustains free-market pricing of drugs and minimizes cost controls …" (Daemmrich 2014, p. A150)

The Cost of Drugs Varies According to Who is Buying

Why It Matters

Different purchasers affect the demand for a therapy in different ways, making decisions about how to price a novel drug complex and unpredictable. Therefore controlling costs necessitates control over several powerful public-sector purchasers, making it an elusive act.

Wholesalers will purchase a product from a pharmaceutical company at a uniform price and resell it to retail pharmacies. Consumers can purchase directly from these retailers at a cost largely reflecting what the uniform price was (without the need for insurance).

Insurers purchase drugs from pharmaceutical companies according to a formula that considers a copayment schedule and also what drugs the insurer decides to cover, and whether that drug is a generic or a "preferred" brand.

Pharmacy Benefit Managers (PBMs) have evolved from administering insurance claims to become negotiators of prices and rebates (if certain sales volumes are reached). They have become controversial as they have grown into ever-larger players in the healthcare ecosystem. They are "hired by many employers and insurers to negotiate drug purchases with pharmacies," and their revenue is a cut of the discounts they broker. Their promoters have promoted the prospect of lower costs for clients through tailored programs and the PBMs' negotiating power. Their detractors have seen them as predatory drivers of ever-higher drug prices and increasingly corporatized healthcare delivery. (Lakdawalla 2018; Mulligan 2022; Robbins and Abelson 2024)

The government (through Medicare Part D and Medicaid) accounts for a large share of the total US pharmaceutical market. This subsidizes the purchase of private insurance and allows such plans to negotiate for lower prices.

Why Different Purchasers Pay Different Prices for Prescription Drugs

An excerpt from a memorandum prepared for the Department of Health and Human Services and presented at a conference on Pharmaceutical Pricing Practices, Utilization and Costs by Anna Cook, PhD

"Pharmaceutical manufacturers of brand-name drugs frequently charge different types of purchasers different prices for the same product. Such price dispersion occurs in markets where suppliers have some degree of market power and purchasers can be separated into groups that vary in their sensitivity to price. In the pharmaceutical industry, variation in price sensitivities across purchasers—combined with patent protection, a large R&D investment, and low production costs—often leads to a wide spectrum of prices for a given pharmaceutical product."

Ironically, patients who pay directly pay the most

"Under this pricing scheme, those purchasers who are uninsured pay the most. In other words, in today's market for outpatient prescription drugs, people who have no insurance coverage for drugs, or third-party payers that do not use a formulary to manage their outpatient drug benefits, pay the highest prices for brand-name drugs. This includes some Medicare beneficiaries with drug coverage under Medigap as well as those who lack drug coverage altogether. Some policymakers have begun to address this issue by incorporating private sector purchasing techniques into proposals to extend a drug benefit to Medicare beneficiaries." (Cook 2000)

In Summary

☞ R&D: While research and development costs are high, the pharmaceutical industry has likely overstated the effect these costs have on drug costs.

☞ Marketing: Director-to-consumer (DTC) marketing and industry-funded physician continuing medical education (CME) programs increase the demand for prescription drugs.

☞ Administration: The pharmaceutical industry engages with a wide array of healthcare regulations, creating a costly administrative framework.

☞ Government: While federal regulations around the development and safety of drugs create administrative costs, the government has historically allowed companies to set prices without regulations. The profit motive creates arbitrarily high costs to insurers and consumers.

6

Government

The US government is on both sides of healthcare cost containment issues. On one side, rising costs have been attributed to increased utilization following the introduction of Medicare and Medicaid. On the other side, the government leads the effort to control costs by negotiating prices and regulating the industry. Either way, its role has proven problematic to the economics of healthcare owing to partisan political ideologies that have limited its power and provided concessions to the industry.

It is true that almost everyone agrees that major healthcare reform is necessary, but such efforts are politically polarizing and tend to succumb to the exigencies of industry influence and legislative wrangling.

❝ *The different elements [of the healthcare system] – employers, employees, doctors, insurance companies, hospitals – all understand what has to be done But they all say they can't do it. There seems to be only one way to get healthcare costs under control. The federal government has to become involved."*

Senator Edward Kennedy in 1976 (Havighurst 1977, p. 471)

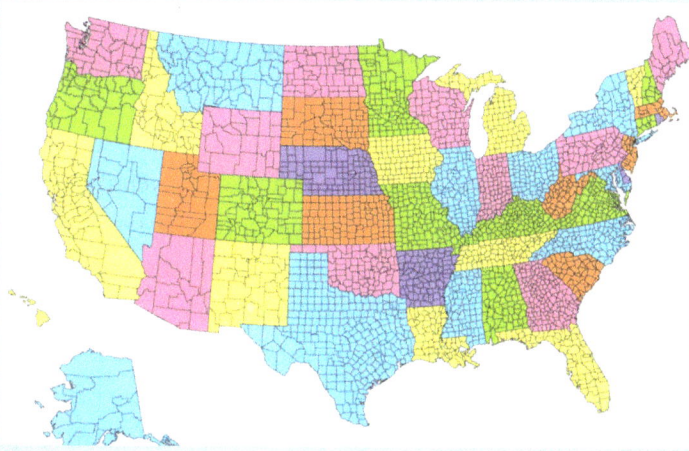

Federal or State?

"Healthcare is a right" has always been a polarizing political theory in the US. Nowhere in the Constitution is there a reference to "health" or "medical care." This has helped inform debates about whether the federal government has any business legislating programs for nation-wide healthcare. In fact, some argue that the Constitution might advise the opposite, with the 10th Amendment giving **states** inherent "police power" to protect public health and safety.

Under this framework, several states have passed laws, amended their state constitutions, or entered into interstate compacts to attempt to "nullify" or "opt out" of the federal individual health insurance mandate and other federal healthcare provisions enacted by the Afford-able Care Act (2010). Direct conflicts between federal laws and state nullification statutes or state constitutional amendments consequently raised constitutional issues that are typically resolved in favor of federal law under the Supremacy Clause of the United States Constitution. Indeed, on June 28, 2012, the Supreme Court upheld the majority of ACA's provisions. (Congressional Research Service 2012)

Can Government Control Healthcare Costs?

A 2014 study evaluated how other nations finance universal healthcare – how they raise revenue, pool risk, negotiate prices for services, and monitor utilization – and how these decisions affect efficiency, cost, and quality of healthcare. The research showed that efficiencies can be reached and costs contained through measures that were developed in the US to help control Medicare costs, namely, prospective payments based on diagnostic related groups. Diverse funding streams to support universal healthcare are more successful than introducing user fees as a means of cost sharing, given the administrative expenses. The 2014 study found that where European countries allow competitive insurance to operate, insurers' incentives to select low risk members leads to cost inequities. (Stabile and Thomson 2014)

Map of countries that provide some form of nationalized healthcare. Most industrialized nations provide universal access to healthcare through nationwide risk pooling financed through income tax.

Government Initiatives Have Worked, At the Expense of Private Sector

The implementation of the Medicare Prospective Payment System (PPS) in 1983 reduced the length of hospital stays of those patients 20% and profits from Medicare billing were decreased, a win for the federal treasury but not for the hospital corporations.

To make up for this, according to the President of the Federation of American Hospitals, hospitals extracted higher payments from their privately insured patients. (Mayes and Hurley 2006)

When employers began to realize that such cost-shifting was occurring, they moved their workers to Health Maintenance Organizations, which accounted for the significant growth of HMOs to the mid 1990s. (Bodenheimer and Grumbach 1995)

The Government is Called Upon When the Market Fails

As Mayes and Hurley (2014) suggest, the growth in HMOs became less about managing care and more about managing costs. Whereas in the late 1980s they successfully lowered premiums, reduced hospital utilization, and negotiated affordable deals for employers, by the mid-1990s their cost control measures were seen as compromising quality, which led to a decline in public support.

Following the failure of the for-profit HMO market to reduce costs and maintain corporate profits, the government was once again invited to the table as an option to provide extended healthcare. (Mayes and Hurley 2014)

The Federal Government Has Intervened in a Piecemeal Way to Provide Healthcare

Under certain circumstances, the laws, regulations, policies, payment systems, and oversight of federal healthcare programs have major direct and indirect influences on private-sector payers and the healthcare that is delivered to Americans not covered under federal programs.

The government's efforts to support disease prevention programs and health promotion aim to reduce healthcare costs. These are areas targeted in the Affordable Care Act's "National Prevention Strategy." (Straube 2013)

That said, attempts at more comprehensive healthcare reform to tackle rising costs, such as by Presidents Harry Truman, Richard Nixon, Jimmy Carter, and Bill Clinton, have failed.

Truman's National Health Bill submitted to Congress in 1945. Image: National Archives, Records of the Committee on Fair Employment Practice

> **"** *The greatest gap in our social security structure is the lack of adequate provision for the Nation's health. We are rightly proud of the high standards of medical care we know how to provide in the United States. The fact is, however, that most of our people cannot afford to pay for the care they need."*

President Truman, State of the Union Address, 1948 (Dolan 2016, p. 15)

The President Cannot Do Everything, But Can Do Nothing

The major efforts of national healthcare reform are predominantly centered on the Office of the President of the United States. This reflects a general problem with the structure of our government and political divisions in Congress. Government has failed to control healthcare costs in part because all presidents deal with many difficult issues and in part because it's high-risk politically.

For decades, policies to rein in healthcare costs were attempted, consistently meeting resistance from the healthcare industry, which was concerned that such efforts would restrict growth and profitability. In the 1970s, Congress imposed rate and review regulations, but it was left to the industry to execute these measures, which failed.

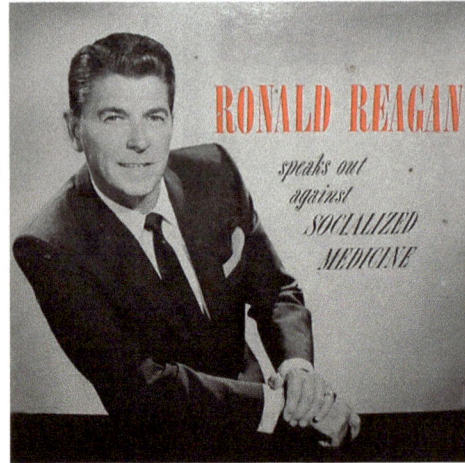

In the 1980s, the Reagan administration believed that market forces would control costs, only to watch national expenditures on healthcare rise to a record 12 percent of the GNP by 1990 (and they continued to rise).

Political Advocates for Nationalized Healthcare Financing Believe it is the Most Economically Efficient Way to Provide Healthcare

Yet, the economic advantage to the nation is a disadvantage to those who profit from healthcare.

When President Bill Clinton took office in 1993 with Democratic majorities in the Senate and House of Representatives, the country appeared inexorably headed toward healthcare reform. It was touted as a balance of public-private involvement in healthcare provision.

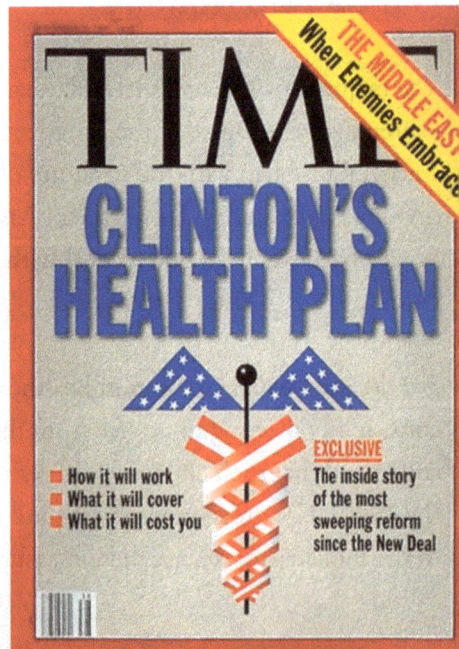

Key provisions of the 1993 Clinton Health Security Act

- Universal coverage and comprehensive benefits
- Mandate that all employers pay 80% of the average health insurance premium for their workers, with caps on total employer costs and subsidies for small businesses
- Cost control through competition with private health plans and federally determined caps on premium increases
- Creation of regional purchasing pools (health alliances) through which people enroll in insurance plans
- Financing through employer mandate, cuts to Medicare and Medicaid, and increase in tobacco taxes (Oberlander 2007)

These reforms would have extended healthcare services to all Americans by changing funding mechanisms and requiring government compensation to insurers that incurred extra costs when accepting high-risk patients.

"inappropriate and premature"

The American Hospital Association, the American Protestant Hospital Association, the Federation of American Health Systems, along with other healthcare industry groups, opposed Clinton's proposals. They claimed that "no such consensus yet exists regarding cost containment," calling the efforts to address the issue "inappropriate and premature." (Wagner 1992)

What went wrong?

- The National Federation of Independent Business vigorously opposed the employer mandate.
- The Health Insurance Association of America fought against insurance regulation and federally imposed cost controls.
- Congressional Republicans denounced the entire plan, including the much-maligned health alliances, as too much "big government."
- Well-insured, middle-class voters preferred the status quo and rejected managed competition (Oberlander 2007) Whereas the "worried well" have been accused of increasing costs by asking for unnecessary medical services (see Chapter 1), the "anxious insured" keep costs high by resisting government-led reforms.

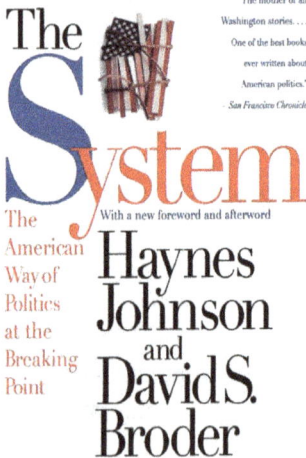

The growing partisanship of American politics in the 1990s played a significant role in the failure of the Clinton healthcare reform initiative. Powerful interest groups, especially the healthcare and insurance lobbies, were a major obstacle to reform. (Johnson and Broder 1996)

The Clinton plan ended up embracing—partly because of pressures from the Congressional Budget Office—strong, centralized, and systemwide cost controls, including premium caps and a national healthcare budget. Cost control measures are what fundamentally drove the effort to begin with, and, paradoxically, are what caused its failure. (Coombs 2005, p. 195)

The
System
"The mother of all Washington stories. . . . One of the best books ever written about American politics."
San Francisco Chronicle

The American Way of Politics at the Breaking Point

With a new foreword and afterword

Haynes Johnson
and
David S. Broder

Alternative Proposals Tear Government Plans Apart

Why It Matters

Despite overwhelming political and popular sentiments that healthcare reform is not only necessary but likely to happen, one study found that too many alternative suggestions, each criticizing another proposal, weakened political momentum and caused failure. (Daniels et al. 1996)

Alongside the Clinton proposal, other healthcare reform proposals were submitted across the political spectrum to the 103rd Congress. One of the most notable alternatives was the single-payer approach, particularly the "American Health Security Act" sponsored by Senator Paul Wellstone and Representative Jim McDermott. Their proposal was modeled after Canada's healthcare system and aimed to provide comprehensive healthcare coverage to all Americans through a single, federally-administered insurance program.

While the single-payer proposal had its supporters, particularly among more progressive members of Congress and various advocacy groups, it did not gain the traction necessary to challenge the Clinton plan as the leading proposal at the time. In the end, neither the Clinton proposal nor the single-payer alternative passed Congress. (Skocpol 1996)

HEARING

BEFORE THE

SUBCOMMITTEE ON LABOR

OF THE

COMMITTEE ON
LABOR AND HUMAN RESOURCES
UNITED STATES SENATE

ONE HUNDRED THIRD CONGRESS

FIRST SESSION

ON

TO PROVIDE FOR A STATE ADMINISTERED SINGLE-PAYER HEALTH
CARE SYSTEM IN THE UNITED STATES, FOCUSING ON ACCESS TO
QUALITY HEALTH CARE AND COST CONTROL ISSUES

OCTOBER 19, 1993

In 1993, Senator Howard Metzenbaum, Chair of the Senate Subcommittee on Labor, opened a hearing on a US single-payer healthcare system by stating:

"Quite simply, a single-payer system is the easiest and fairest type of healthcare system. All that single-payer means is that instead of 1,500 insurance companies, a single entity collects our healthcare dollars and directly pays healthcare providers. Under a single-payer system, Government raises the revenue either through income or payroll taxes, and providers of healthcare determine how these funds will be spent. Single-payer requires the least amount of government bureaucracy, while providing doctors and patients with the maximum amount of free choice and flexibility. What single-payer doesn't have is the middle-man – no more insurance companies, no more claims reviewers. Nor is single-payer the system for multimillionaire doctors."
(Subcommittee on Labor 1994, p. 2)

Economic Interests Control Political Action

Why It Matters

Other than national security, government efforts to provide universal protections to US citizens are strongly resisted, and often defeated, because they are seen as a threat to profits.

Too many people profit from the current costly system and mount campaigns against change. As articulated by professor of social medicine and health policy at UNC Chapel Hill, Jonathan Oberlander: "Thus, although everyone decries the amount of money spent on healthcare, the political reality is that national healthcare expenditures represent income to health industry stakeholders, whose interests lie in ensuring even greater spending." (Oberlander 2007)

Publicly traded, for-profit corporations that dominate the financing and delivery of healthcare have, in very practical aspects, created the biggest barrier to reform. More philosophically, the idea that healthcare problems will be solved by market forces has dominated decision making.

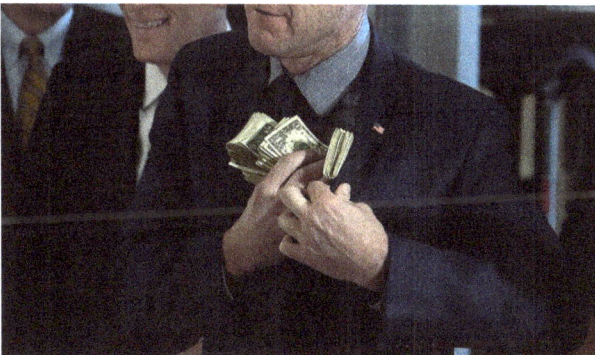

Government Plans for Health Reform Suffer Constant Attack by Industry Lobbyists

Interest groups promoting the interests of for-profit businesses launch campaigns such as the notorious Harry and Louise ads – funded by the Health Insurance Association of America – that portrayed Clinton's reforms as healthcare "run by tens of thousands of new bureaucrats." (Coombs 2005)

"Our deep distrust of central government control, coupled with our profound faith in the moral precepts of commerce and the market, our driving need for personal autonomy, and our occasional spasms of intense partisanship, have frustrated our best efforts at system improvement." (Dr. Frank Davidoff and Dr. Robert Reinecke, in Coombs 2005, p. 261)

AHIP

America's Health
Insurance Plans

America's Health Insurance Plans (AHIP) represents insurance providers offering all types of health coverage, including Medicare Advantage and employer-based programs. The organization spent $9.5 million in 2019 on federal lobbying. (Source: OpenSecrets.org)

When Government Concedes Oversight to Industry, Costs Increase

Why It Matters

In compromises to attain bipartisan or industry support for reform, structural flaws are deliberately introduced into laws that make them functionally inefficient.

Because almost *any* piece of major legislation is going to require bipartisan support, necessitating compromise between supporters and opponents of the proposal, opponents will introduce a way to structure the program that ensures it cannot succeed. (Moe 1990)

Fraud and Abuse: A Government Invitation

Not long after the 1966 enactment of Medicare and Medicaid, evidence emerged that unscrupulous physicians and healthcare organizations were gaming the system. Research over the past 50 years shows that around 10 percent of the federal government's annual cost for these programs is attributed to fraudulent claims or abuses where hospitals and treatments have been overused for undue provider profit.

In drafting and debating amendments to the Social Security Act (where Medicare laws were embedded), and in an effort to prevent their derailment through nonparticipation or physician strikes, lawmakers spelled out the limits of the government's powers to interfere with the business of providing healthcare. One of the first paragraphs of the Medicare Act (1965), Section 1801, is titled "Prohibition Against Any Federal Interference," stating that the law does not permit "any supervision or control over the administration or operation" of the program. (Dolan and Beitler 2022, p. 480)

Government Actions Are Driven By Popular Opinion And Not Scientific Data

Why It Matters

The government acts in the best interests of legislators who are heavily influenced, and funded, by industry groups.

In Brief

In 2008, the lobbying group AHIP tapped the consulting firm APCO to develop an effort to label any government-run insurance option as an existential threat to democratic political goals. The campaign adopted a two-pronged strategy: position private health insurance as the only positive solution to America's healthcare woes and "disqualify government-run healthcare as a politically viable solution."

The same group was activated in 2018 to discredit the idea of "Medicare for All."

Despite polls showing significant popularity for single-payer coverage, private healthcare interests developed plans to influence Democratic Party messaging and stymie the momentum toward achieving universal healthcare coverage. Popular opinion was shaped by opposition messaging that the government was bad for healthcare, leaving the market and private interests to control costs. (Fang and Surgey 2018)

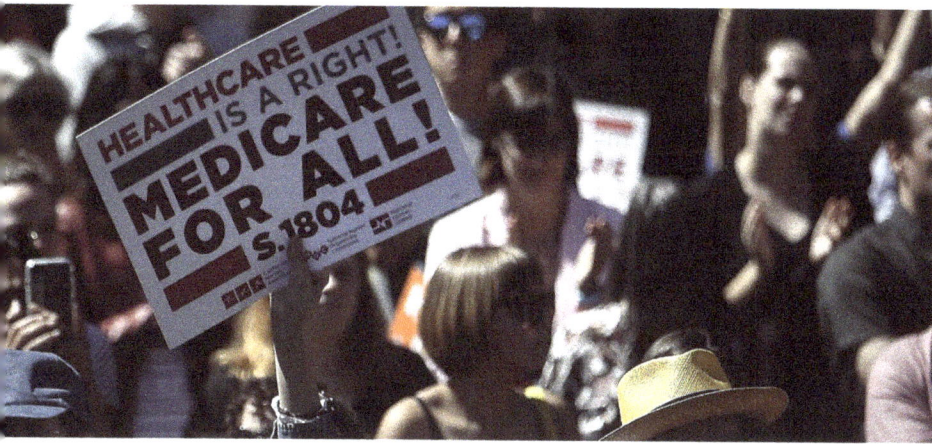

The Joke Is On Legislators – The Industry Bets On Policy Failures

Why It Matters

The industry sees high costs as revenue streams, and political measures to control costs as doomed to fail largely because of inevitable concessions to the industry itself. Without a coordinated effort to reduce overall costs, and with one side anticipating the failure of the other side's measures, costs will not be contained.

"Bureaucrats in DC have no understanding of a person's medical situation and will be making decisions about your healthcare instead of doctors."

Political lobbyist group Partnership for America's Healthcare Future talking point in the lead-up to the 2020 elections.

Stock prices reflect investors' expectations about the effectiveness of proposed cost-control measures. An effective government-driven cost-containment policy would be viewed as an adverse development for the health sector, pushing investors to shift their investments to more attractive industries, causing stock prices of health firms to decline. Examining the reaction of investors (reflected in stock activity) to proposed legislation aiming to reduce healthcare costs has revealed that **the industry anticipates political failure**. (Jacobson 1994)

If industry lobbyists opposed cost containment measures out of concern over threats to their growth and profitability, repeated failures of such legislation have diminished their concerns that the government would ever succeed.

Health care vs. S&P 500

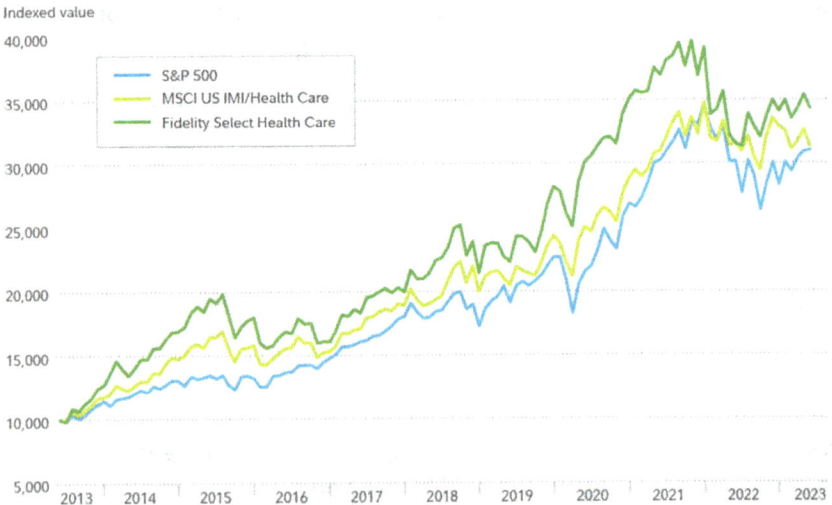

Indexed value

Legend:
- S&P 500
- MSCI US IMI/Health Care
- Fidelity Select Health Care

Cost Control Compromises Helped Pass the Affordable Care Act (ACA) of 2010

The Obama administration learned lessons from past failures and dropped elements that had caused such concern.

For example, the Obama administration sought to exempt small businesses from any mandate and reassure Americans who were happy with their insurance that they could keep their plans. More importantly, the ACA avoided proposals for budgeting or imposing systemwide price controls, favoring targeted cost-saving mechanisms like electronic health records and, more controversially, by raising money through taxation.

The ACA was forged through "political pragmatism" and by conceding divisive issues such as government-funded abortion, comprehensive benefits, and a commitment to universal coverage (pushing instead for "near universal" coverage). (Oberlander 2010)

Financing Streams of the Affordable Care Act

"The ACA included multiple streams of financing that were intended not only to support new spending obligations such as Medicaid expansion and health insurance subsidies, but also to change both healthcare and health insurance incentive structures and to magnify the law's redistributive effects. Some financing sources were imposed on healthcare stakeholders, such as new annual fees on pharmaceutical manufacturers and health insurers as well as taxes on medical devices and indoor tanning services. More relevant for possible social, political, or economic effects were tax changes for individuals, ranging from lower limits on flexible spending accounts for medical expenses and an increased threshold for itemized deduction of unreimbursed medical expenses, to changes with clearly redistributive implications, such as increased capital gains and Medicare payroll taxes for high earners and the so-called Cadillac tax.

"Among the financing streams, the Cadillac tax was the subject of the most hypothesizing and analysis. A 40 percent excise tax on employer-sponsored health benefits that exceed certain thresholds, the Cadillac tax was intended not only to raise revenue but also to partly offset the tax exclusion for employer-sponsored insurance and to discourage employers from offering health plans that are so comprehensive that they encourage overuse." (Excerpt from Campbell and Shore-Sheppard 2020, pp. 9-10)

Did the Affordable Care Act Reduce the Affordability of Healthcare?

As the ACA increased the number of individuals covered by health insurance, the history of Medicare and Medicaid suggested that the healthcare system again would see an influx of new users. Health economists projected that this increased demand would impact the supply of doctors, nurses, technicians, and home health aides. Labor shortages drive up wages, in turn causing a rise in reimbursements and insurance premiums. (Parente et al. 2017) However, the coincidence of the ACA's passage with the start of an economic recovery makes analyses of wage changes difficult to attribute to a particular cause.

Researchers have also studied the impact of competition on consumer prices in the ACA's individual insurance market, finding that the entry of an additional insurer generally resulted in a reduction in prices to consumers of between 4 and 5 percent. (Campbell and Shore-Sheppard 2020)

Yes and No?

➤ By expanding insurance coverage, such as through Medicaid expansion under the ACA, more people access services, leading to an increase in total health spending, but potentially reducing costs per person or shifting costs from uncompensated care.

In Summary

The experience of other nations with government-run healthcare systems shows that there are several potential strategies for lowering costs in America:

Price Caps
Some countries set price limits for certain medical services or products, such as prescription drugs, to ensure they remain affordable.

Bulk Purchasing
Governments might negotiate drug prices or use their purchasing power to achieve discounts on medical products or services.

Quality Control and Efficiency
Regulations aimed at improving the quality of care can lead to better health outcomes, potentially reducing the need for further treatment and associated costs.

Preventive Care
Mandates for insurance plans to cover preventive services without out-of-pocket costs can potentially reduce costs in the long term by catching diseases early or preventing them altogether.

Generic Drug Promotion
By facilitating the entry of generic drugs into the market, governments can reduce medication costs.

Conclusion

When people find out that you're studying healthcare costs, you hear this a lot:

"So why does it cost so much?"

We would nominate two main factors. First, America has grafted healthcare delivery, organization, and funding onto an economic structure that doesn't fit well. Some features, such as fee-for-service billing and a major role for profit-driven insurers, can be good for doctors and shareholders, but they have discouraged cost-effectiveness and have not produced better health results.

Over the last 50 years, American patients have also paid their share, through taxes and insurance premiums, for the growing financialization of healthcare. Pharmaceutical companies, hospitals, device manufacturers, and other healthcare sector participants have exploited a poor economic fit to increase market and political power in a self-reinforcing loop that rewards shareholders while driving prices higher.

Second is the control of medical knowledge — among doctors and patients — by commercial interests. Even top-tier medical journals, it turns out, are not immune to financial inducements. In addition, as wider swaths of many medical specialties are colonized by private-equity firms, the data that doctors rely on is increasingly curated to advance financial goals.

These conclusions are not novel with us, and many highly informed critiques of our healthcare system are available. In *Sickening* (2022), physician and policy scholar John Abramson detailed how the control of medical information shapes doctors' practices and patients' understandings. In *Fragmented* (2023), Ilana Yurkiewicz, an oncologist and internal medicine physician, depicted in vivid clinical detail how obstacles to continuity in treatment harm patients, undermine doctors, and waste money. In *Big Med* (2021), management scholars David Dranove and Lawton R. Burns wrote:

"Large, integrated hospital-based systems – we call them megaproviders – bear the greatest responsibility for the cost and quality of medical care: more than drug companies, more than insurers, more than the government."

Elisabeth Rosenthal's dual perspective as physician and journalist made *An American Sickness: How Healthcare Became Big Business and How You Can Take It Back* (2017) both wide-ranging and specific as it skewered waste, irrationality, and danger across the system. In *Bad Pharma: How Drug Companies Mislead Doctors and Harm Patients* (2013), physician Benjamin Goldacre, based in Britain, focused on the data that most physicians, and virtually all their patients, ever see. Clinical trial data that don't support a marketing plan, said Goldacre, have a way of disappearing.

By themselves, these and other diverse critiques of American healthcare suggest complex historical roots of today's costs. What unites these analyses is the idea that high healthcare costs are not an accident. Our costs are the product of choices and decisions made in government agencies, doctors' offices, people's homes, and corporate offices. They are the outcome of policy roads taken, abandoned, or never broached. They have been forged by power – in markets, in the culture, and in politics –

whose growth has been a goal, and now an achievement, of commercial and professional interests.

And if high costs are not a fluke, then lowering them, or at least slowing their growth, won't be either. Such solutions will require courage, creativity, and an appetite for big changes across the healthcare ecosystem.

The last 100 years don't inspire much hope that we will make healthcare less costly. But those years haven't made it impossible either. The history of medicine teems with examples of how people and groups achieved what the conventional wisdom said would not happen.

Who knows?

In 100 years, historians might say the 2020s were when America began to reverse the tide of ever-higher healthcare costs.

No matter what those historians conclude, we wish you good health.

Bibliography

Abramson, John. *Sickening: How Big Pharma Broke American Health Care and How We Can Repair It*. How Big Pharma Broke American Health Care and How We Can Repair It. Boston; Mariner Books, 2022.

Adams, Richard. "Pay Medical Bills with a Chicken, Says Republican Candidate." *The Guardian*, April 21, 2010. https://www.theguardian.com/world/richard-adams-blog/2010/apr/21/sue-lowden-lowden-care-chickens-nevada.

Allen, Lindsay. "The Inflation Reduction Act: Hope for Prescription Drug Prices in the USA," *Applied Health Economics and Health Policy*, 22 (online 2023; print 2024) 5-7.

Altomare, Ivy, Blair Irwin, Syed Yousuf Zafar, Kevin Houck, Bailey Maloney, Rachel Greenup, Jeffrey Peppercorn, Ivy Altomare, Blair Irwin, and Syed Yousuf Zafar. "ReCAP: Physician Experience and Attitudes toward Addressing the Cost of Cancer Care." *Journal of Oncology Practice* 12, no. 3 (2016): 247–48.

American Medical Association. "Committee on Hygiene and Public Health." *Journal of the American Medical Association* 74, no. 19 (1920): 1319.

Appel, Toby A. "The Thomsonian Movement, the Regular Profession, and the State in Antebellum Connecticut: A Case Study of the Repeal of Early Medical Licensing Laws." *Journal of the History of Medicine and Allied Sciences* 65, no. 2 (April 1, 2010): 153–86. https://doi.org/10.1093/jhmas/jrp035.

Arora, Vineet, Christopher Moriates, and Neel Shah. "The Challenge of Understanding Health Care Costs and Charges." *AMA Journal of Ethics* 17, no. 11 (2015): 1046–52.

Arrow, Kenneth J. "Uncertainty and The Welfare Economics of Medical Care." *Journal of Health Politics, Policy and Law* 26, no. 5 (2001): 851–83. https://doi.org/10.1215/03616878-26-5-851.

Bach, Peter. "Could High Drug Prices Be Bad For Innovation?" *Forbes*, October 23, 2014.

Barocci, Thomas. *Non-Profit Hospitals: Their Structure, Human Resources, and Economic Importance*. Boston: Auburn House Publishing Company, 1981.

Bartz, Robert J. "Generalists First: The Movement to Refashion General Practice in Post-World War II America." Thesis (Ph.D.)--University of California, San Francisco, 2005., 2005.

Baum, Aaron, Zirui Song, Bruce E. Landon, Russell S. Phillips, Asaf Bitton, and Sanjay Basu. "Health Care Spending Slowed After Rhode Island Applied Affordability Standards to Commercial Insurers." *Health Affairs* 38, no. 2 (February 1, 2019): 237–45. https://doi.org/10.1377/hlthaff.2018.05164.

Becker, Gay, Rahima Jan Gates, and Edwina Newsom. "Self-Care Among Chronically Ill African Americans: Culture, Health Disparities, and Health Insurance Status." *American Journal of Public Health (1971)* 94, no. 12 (2004): 2066–73. https://doi.org/10.2105/AJPH.94.12.2066.

Blackburn, Julia, Stefan Fischerauer, Moitaba Talaei-Khoei, Neal Chen, Luke Oh, and Ana-Maria Vranceanu. "What Are the Implications of Excessive Internet Searches for Medical Information by Orthopaedic Patients?" *Clinical Orthopaedics and Related Research* 477, no. 12 (2019): 2665–73. https://doi.org/10.1097/CORR.0000000000000888.

Blendon, Robert J, and John M Benson. "Americans' Views On Health Policy: A Fifty-Year Historical Perspective." *Health Affairs* 20, no. 2 (2001): 33–46. https://doi.org/10.1377/hlthaff.20.2.33.

Blendon, Robert J., Molllyann Brodie, John M. Benson, Drew E. Altman, and Tami Buhr. "Americans' Views of Health Care Costs, Access, and Quality." *Milbank Quarterly* 84, no. 4 (December 2006): 623–57.

Blumenthal, David, and James A Morone. *The Heart of Power: Health and Politics in the Oval Office.* University of California Press, 2010. https://doi.org/10.1525/j.ctt1pnrr6.

Boccuti, Cristina, and Marilyn Moon. "Comparing Medicare and Private Insurers: Growth Rates in Spending over Three Decades." *Health Affairs* 22, no. 2 (2003): 230–37.

Bodenheimer, Thomas. "Should We Abolish the Private Health Insurance Industry?" *International Journal of Health Services* 20, no. 2 (1990): 199–220. https://doi.org/10.2190/DAKX-ULL1-R1EF-X5NR.

Bodenheimer, Thomas, and Kevin Grumbach. "The Reconfiguration of US Medicine." *Journal of the American Medical Association* 274, no. 1 (1995): 85–90.

Boyd, Eddie L, Stephanie D Taylor, Leslie A Shimp, and Colleen R Semler. "An Assessment of Home Remedy Use by African Americans." *Journal of the National Medical Association* 92, no. 7 (2000): 341.

Branning, Gary, and Martha Vater. "Healthcare Spending: Plenty of Blame to Go Around." *American Health Drug Benefits* 9, no. 8 (2016): 445–47.

Brick, Danielle J., Karen A. Scherr, and Peter A. Ubel. "The Impact of Cost Conversations on the Patient-Physician Relationship." *Health Communication* 34, no. 1 (January 2, 2019): 65–73. https://doi.org/10.1080/10410236.2017.1384428.

Brook, Robert H., Emmett B. Keeler, Kathleen N. Lohr, Joseph P. Newhouse, John E. Ware, William H. Rogers, Allyson Ross Davies, et al. *The Health Insurance Experiment: A Classic RAND Study Speaks to the Current Health Care Reform Debate*. Santa Monica, CA: RAND Corporation, 2006. https://www.rand.org/pubs/research_briefs/RB9174.html.

Brownlee, Shannon. *Overtreated: Why Too Much Medicine is Making Us Sicker and Poorer*. New York: Bloomsbury, 2008.

Budrys, Grace. *Market-Based Health Care: All Myth, No Reality*. Rowman & Littlefield, 2019.

Byrd, W. Michael, and Linda A. Clayton, eds. *An American Health Dilemma: Volume II: Race, Medicine, and Health Care in the United States, 1900-2000*. New York: Routledge, 2002.

Caldwell, Bert W. "The Cost of Medical Care from the Viewpoint of the Hospital." In *Hospitals and the Cost of Medical Care*, Vol. American Conference of Hospital Service February 18, 1930. Chicago: American Hospital Association, 1930.

Califano, Joseph. *America's Health Care Revolution: Who Lives? Who Dies? Who Pays?* New York: Random House, 1986.

Callahan, Daniel, and Angela Wasunna. *Medicine and the Market: Equity V. Choice*. Baltimore: Johns Hopkins University Press, 2006.

Calvo, Rocio, Joanna M Jablonska-Bayro, and Mary C Waters. "Obamacare in Action: How Access to the Health Care System Contributes to Immigrants' Sense of Belonging." *Journal of Ethnic and Migration Studies* 43, no. 12 (2017): 2020–36.

Campbell, Andrea Louise, and Lara Shore-Sheppard. "The Social, Political, and Economic Effects of the Affordable Care Act: Introduction to the Issue." *RSF: The Russell Sage Foundation Journal of the Social Sciences* 6, no. 2 (2020): 1–40. https://doi.org/10.7758/RSF.2020.6.2.01.

Carpenter, Eugenia S., and Pamela Paul-Shaheen. "Implementing Regu-

latory Reform: The Saga of Michigan's Debedding Experiment."
  Journal of Health Politics, Policy and Law 9, no. 3 (June 1, 1984):
  453–73. https://doi.org/10.1215/03616878-9-3-453.

Center for Medicare and Medicaid Services. "Market Rating Reform."
  CMS.gov, n.d. https://www.cms.gov/CCIIO/Programs-and-Initia-
  tives/Health-Insurance-Market-Reforms/Market-Rating-Reforms.

Center for Public Integrity (CPI). 2016a. "Pharma lobbying held deep
  influence over opioid policies." September 18, 2016. https://pub-
  licintegrity.org/state-politics/pharma-lobbying-held-deep-influ-
  ence-over-opioid-policies/.

Center for Public Integrity (CPI) 2016b. "Politics of pain: Drugmakers
  fought state opioid limits amid crisis." December 15, 2016. www.
  publicintegrity.org/2016/09/18/20200/politics-pain-drugmakers-
  fought-state-opioid-limits-amid-crisis.

Chernew, Michael, and Harrison Mintz. "Administrative Expenses in
  the US Health Care System: Why So High?" *JAMA* 326, no.
  17 (November 2, 2021): 1679–80. https://doi.org/10.1001/
  jama.2021.17318.

Codman, Ernest A. "The Product of a Hospital." *Surg Gynecol Obstet.* 18
  (1914): 491–96.

Cohn, Jonathan. *Sick: The Untold Story of America's Health Care Crisis--and
  the People Who Pay the Price.* HarperCollins Publishers New York,
  2007.

Collins, Sara R, Petra W Rasmussen, Michelle M Doty, and Sophie Beutel.
  "The Rise in Health Care Coverage and Affordability since Health
  Reform Took Effect: Findings from the Commonwealth Fund Bi-
  ennial Health Insurance Survey, 2014." *Issue Brief (Commonwealth
  Fund)* 2 (2015): 1–16.

Comptroller General of the United States. *Health Care Facilities Construction Costs.* Washington, D.C.: U.S. Government Printing Office,
  1972.

Congressional Budget Office. "Research and Development in the Pharmaceutical Industry." Washington, D.C., April 2021. www.cbo.gov/
  publication/57025.

Congressional Research Service. "Health Care: Constitutional Rights and
  Legislative Powers," July 9, 2012. www.crs.gov.

Cook, Anna. "Why Different Purchasers Pay Different Prices for Prescription Drugs," A memorandum prepared for the Department

of Health and Human Services. Conference on Pharmaceutical Pricing Practices, Utilization and Costs. August 8-9, 2000. https://aspe.hhs.gov/why-different-purchasers-pay-different-prices-pre-scription-drugs

Coombs, Jan Gregoire. *The Rise and Fall of HMOs: An American Health Care Revolution.* Madison, WI: The University of Wisconsin Press, 2005.

Council of Economic Advisors. "The Profitability of Health Insurance Companies." Executive Office of the President of the United States, March 2018. https://trumpwhitehouse.archives.gov/wp-content/uploads/2018/03/The-Profitability-of-Health-Insurance-Compa-nies.pdf.

Crenner, Christopher. *Private Practice In the Early Twentieth-Century Medical Office of Dr. Richard Cabot.* Baltimore and London: Johns Hopkins University Press, 2005.

Crooks, Valorie A., Paul Kingsbury, Jeremy Snyder, and Rory Johnston. "What Is Known about the Patient's Experience of Medical Tour-ism? A Scoping Review." *BMC Health Services Research* 10, no. 1 (September 8, 2010): 266. https://doi.org/10.1186/1472-6963-10-266.

Cunningham, Robert, and Robert M. (Robert Maris) Cunningham. *The Blues : A History of the Blue Cross and Blue Shield System.* DeKalb: Northern Illinois University Press, 1997.

Cutler, David M., and Richard J. Zeckhauser. "Chapter 11 - The Anatomy of Health Insurance* *We Are Grateful to Dan Altman for Research Assistance, to Jon Gruber, Tom McGuire, Joe Newhouse, and Alexandra Sidorenko for Helpful Comments, and to the National Institutes on Aging for Research Support." In *Handbook of Health Economics*, edited by Anthony J. Culyer and Joseph P. Newhouse, 1:563–643. Elsevier, 2000. https://doi.org/10.1016/S1574-0064(00)80170-5.

Daemmrich, Arthur and Ansuman Mohanty. "Healthcare Reform in the United States and China: Pharmaceutical Market Implications," *Journal of Pharm Policy Practice* 14 (2014), 9.

Dafny, Leemore. "Evaluating the Impact of Health Insurance Industry Con-solidation: Learning From Experience." The CommonWealth Fund, November 20, 2015.

Daniels, Norman, Donald W. Light, and Ronald Caplan. *Benchmarks of*

Fairness for Health Care Reform. New York: Oxford University Press, 1996.

DiMasi, Joseph A, Ronald W Hansen, Henry G Grabowski, and Louis Lasagna. "Cost of Innovation in the Pharmaceutical Industry." *Journal of Health Economics* 10, no. 2 (1991): 107–42. https://doi.org/10.1016/0167-6296(91)90001-4.

Dolan, Brian. "Socialism, Medicine, and the Yoke of European Dictatorship." *Medical History for Medical Students*, 2016. http://ucmedicalhumanitiespress.com/magazines/socialism-medicare-and-the-yoke-of-european-dictatorship/.

Dolan, Brian, and Stephen Beitler. "Legislating Medicare Fraud: The Politics of Self-Regulation and the Creation of Professional Standards Review Organizations." *Journal of Policy History* 34, no. 4 (2022): 475–504.

Donelan, Karen, Robert J Blendon, Cathy Schoen, Karen Davis, and Katherine Binns. "The Cost Of Health System Change: Public Discontent In Five Nations: Amid Widely Divergent Systems and Cultural Norms of Health Care, Citizens Express Surprisingly Similar Concerns about the Future." *Health Affairs* 18, no. 3 (1999): 206–16.

Donohue, Julie. "A History of Drug Advertising: The Evolving Roles of Consumers and Consumer Protection." *The Milbank Quarterly* 84, no. 4 (2006): 659–99.

Dranove, David. *The Economic Evolution of American Healthcare.* Princeton: Princeton University Press, 2000.

Dranove, David and Lawton Robert Burns. *Big Med: Megaproviders and the High Cost of Health Care in America.* Chicago: University of Chicago Press, 2021.

Eilers, Robert Dale. *Regulation of Blue Cross and Blue Shield Plans.* University of Pennsylvania, 1961.

Eisenberg, John M, and Arnold J Rosoff. "Physician Responsibility for the Cost of Unnecessary Medical Services." *New England Journal of Medicine* 299, no. 2 (1978): 76–80.

Enthoven, Alain C. *Health Plan: The Only Practical Solution to the Soaring Cost of Medical Care.* Reading, Mass: Addison-Wesley Pub. Co., 1980.

Epstein, Arnold M., Colin B. Begg, and Barbara J. McNeil. "The Use of Ambulatory Testing in Prepaid and Fee-for-Service Group Practices." *New England Journal of Medicine* 314, no. 17 (April 24, 1986): 1089–94. https://doi.org/10.1056/NEJM198604243141706.

Fang, Lee, and Nick Surgey. "Lobbyist Documents Reveal Health Care Industry Battle Plan Against 'Medicare for All.'" *The Intercept*, November 20, 2018. https://theintercept.com/2018/11/20/medi-care-for-all-healthcare-industry/.

Finkelstein, Amy. *Moral Hazard in Health Insurance.* New York: Columbia University Press, 2015.

Fletcher, Rebecca Adkins. "Keeping up with the Cadillacs: What Health Insurance Disparities, Moral Hazard, and the Cadillac Tax Mean to The Patient Protection and Affordable Care Act." *Medical Anthropology Quarterly* 30, no. 1 (March 1, 2016): 18–36. https://doi.org/10.1111/maq.12120.

Fonda, Daren, Anne Berryman, Alice Jackson-Baughn, and Leslie Whitaker. "Sick of Hospital Bills." *Time*, September 27, 2004. http://content.time.com/time/subscriber/printout/0,8816,995200,00.html.

Friedman, Milton. "How to Cure Health Care." *The Public Interest*, 2001, 3.

Friedson, Andrew. *Economics of Healthcare: A Brief Introduction.* Cambridge: Cambridge University Press, 2023.

Fuchs, V. R. "Managed Care and Merger Mania." *JAMA : The Journal of the American Medical Association* 277, no. 11 (1997): 920–21. https://doi.org/10.1001/jama.277.11.920.

Fuchs, Victor R. "Managed Care and Merger Mania." *JAMA* 277, no. 11 (1997): 920–21.

Gainty, Caitjan. "The Autobiographical Shoulder of Ernest Amory Codman: Crafting Medical Meaning in the Twentieth Century." *Bulletin of the History of Medicine* 90, no. 3 (2016): 394–423. https://doi.org/10.1353/bhm.2016.0071.

Garfield, Sidney R. "The Delivery of Medical Care." *Scientific American* 222, no. 4 (1970): 15–23.

Gaynor, Martin., and Gerard F. Anderson. "Hospital Costs and the Cost of Empty Hospital Beds." NBER Working Paper. Cambridge, MA: National Bureau of Economic Research, 1991. https://www.nber.org/papers/w3872.

Gee, Emily, and Topher Spiro. "Excess Administrative Costs Burden the U.S. Health Care System." Center for American Progress, April 8, 2019.

———. "Excessive Administrative Costs Burden the U.S. Health Care

System." Center for American Progress, April 8, 2019. https://www.americanprogress.org/article/excess-administrative-costs-burden-u-s-health-care-system/.

Geiger, William J, and Ronald A Krol. "Physician Attitudes and Behavior in Response to Changes in Medicare Reimbursement Policies." *J Fam Pract* 33, no. 3 (1991): 244–48.

Ginsburg, Marjorie E, Richard L Kravitz, and William A Sandberg. "A Survey of Physician Attitudes and Practices Concerning Cost-Effectiveness in Patient Care." *Western Journal of Medicine* 173, no. 6 (2000): 390.

Glasziou, Paul, Sharon Straus, Shannon Brownlee, Lyndal Trevena, Leonila Dans, Gordon Guyatt, et al. "Evidence for Underuse of Effective Medical Services Around the World," *The Lancet* 390: 10090 (2017), pp. 169-177. https://www.thelancet.com/journals/lancet/article/PIIS0140-6736(16)30946-1/abstract

Goldacre, Ben. *Bad Pharma : How Drug Companies Mislead Doctors and Harm Patients.* First American edition. New York: Faber and Faber, Inc., an affiliate of Farrar, Straus and Giroux, 2013.

Goody, B, M A Friedman, and W Sobaski. "New Directions for Medicare Payment Systems." *Health Care Financing Review* 16, no. 2 (1994): 1–11.

Gray, Bradford H. *For-Profit Enterprise in Health Care.* Washington, D.C: National Academy Press, 1986.

Gray, Bradford H. *The Profit Motive and Patient Care: The Changing Accountability of Doctors and Hospitals.* Harvard University Press, 1991.

Gunja, Munira, Evan Gumas, and Reginald Williams II. "U.S. Health Care from a Global Perspective, 2022: Accelerating Spending, Worsening Outcomes." The CommonWealth Fund, January 31, 2023. https://www.commonwealthfund.org/publications/issue-briefs/2023/jan/us-health-care-global-perspective-2022.

Guterman, S, and A Dobson. "Impact of the Medicare Prospective Payment System for Hospitals." *Health Care Financing Review* 7, no. 3 (1986): 97–114.

———. "Impact of the Medicare Prospective Payment System for Hospitals." *Health Care Financing Review* 7, no. 3 (1986): 97–114.

Hadland, Scott E., Maxwell S. Krieger, and Brandon D. L. Marshall. "Industry Payments to Physicians for Opioid Products, 2013-

2015." *American Journal of Public Health (1971)* 107, no. 9 (2017): 1493–95. https://doi.org/10.2105/AJPH.2017.303982.

Hadley, Jack, Stephen Zuckerman, and Judith Feder. "Profits and Fiscal Pressure in the Prospective Payment System: Their Impacts on Hospitals." *Inquiry* 26, no. 3 (1989): 354–65.

Hannick, Kathleen. "5 Things to Understand About Pharmaceutical R&D." Commentary. *USC-Brookings Schaeffer Initiative for Health Policy*, June 2, 2022. https://www.brookings.edu/articles/five-things-to-understand-about-pharmaceutical-rd/.

Hansmann, Henry B. "The Role of Nonprofit Enterprise." *Yale LJ* 89 (1979): 835.

Harmon, Gerald. Gerald Harmon, MD, on physicians' role in a pandemic of mistrust, February 1, 2022. https://www.ama-assn.org/delivering-care/public-health/gerald-harmon-md-physicians-role-pandemic-mistrust.

Havighurst, Clark C. "Controlling Health Care Costs: Strengthening the Private Sector's Hand." *Journal of Health Politics, Policy and Law* 1, no. 4 (August 1, 1977): 471–98. https://doi.org/10.1215/03616878-1-4-471.

Hero, Joachim O, Alan M Zaslavsky, and Robert J Blendon. "The United States Leads Other Nations in Differences by Income in Perceptions of Health and Health Care." *Health Affairs* 36, no. 6 (2017): 1032–40.

Hilts, Philip. *Protecting America's Health: The FDA, Business, and One Hundred Years of Regulation*. New York: Alfred A. Knopf, 2003.

Himmelstein, David U., Terry Campbell, and Steffie Woolhandler. "Health Care Administrative Costs in the United States and Canada, 2017." *Annals of Internal Medicine* 172, no. 2 (January 21, 2020): 134–42. https://doi.org/10.7326/M19-2818.

Hollander, Mara A. G., Julie M. Donohue, Bradley D. Stein, Elizabeth E. Krans, and Marian P. Jarlenski. "Association between Opioid Prescribing in Medicare and Pharmaceutical Company Gifts by Physician Specialty." *Journal of General Internal Medicine: JGIM* 35, no. 8 (2020): 2451–58. https://doi.org/10.1007/s11606-019-05470-0.

Hornbrook, Mark C. "Review Article: Hospital Case Mix: Its Definition, Measurement and Use: Part I. The Conceptual Framework." *Medical Care Review* 39, no. 1 (March 1, 1982): 1–43. https://doi.org/10.1177/107755878203900101.

Hughes, Robert G., and Harold S. Luft. "Service Patterns in Local Hospital Markets: Complementarity or Medical Arms Race?" *Health Services Management Research* 4, no. 2 (July 1, 1991): 131–39. https://doi.org/10.1177/095148489100400206.

Institute of Medicine. *Reliability of Hospital Discharge Abstracts: Report of a Study, February, 1977.* Publication IOM ; 77-01. Washington: National Academy of Sciences, 1977.

Interlandi, Jeneen. "Why Doesn't the United States Have Universal Health Care? The Answer Has Everything to Do With Race." *The New York Times Magazine*, August 14, 2019. https://www.nytimes.com/interactive/2019/08/14/magazine/universal-health-care-racism.html.

Jacobson, Carol. "Investor Response to Health Care Cost Containment Legislation: Is American Health Policy Designed to Fail?" *Academy of Management Journal* 37, no. 2 (1994): 440–52.

Jeurissen, Patrick, Florien Kruse, Reinhard Busse, David Himmelstein, Elias Mossialos, Steffie Woolhander. "For-Profit Hospitals Have Thrived Because of Generous Public Reimbursement Schemes, Not Greater Efficiency: A Multi-Country Case Study." *International Journal of Health Services* 51:1 (2021): 67-89. doi: 10.1177/0020731420966976

Johnson, Carolyn, and Brady Dennis. "How An $84,000 Drug Got Its Price: 'Let's Hold Our Position ... Whatever the Headlines.'" *Washington Post*, December 1, 2015.

Johnson, Haynes, and David Broder. *The System: The American Way of Politics at the Breaking Point.* New York: Little, Brown, 1996.

Jorgensen, Paul D. "Pharmaceuticals, Political Money, and Public Policy: A Theoretical and Empirical Agenda," *The Journal of Law, Medicine, and Ethics* 41:3 (2013), 561-570.

Karpman, Michael. "Most Adults With Past-Due Medical Debt Owe Money to Hospitals." Urban Institute, March 2023.

King, Lester S. "Medicine—Trade or Profession?" *JAMA* 253, no. 18 (May 10, 1985): 2709–10. https://doi.org/10.1001/jama.1985.03350420121031.

Kluender, Raymond, Neale Mahoney, Francis Wong, and Wesley Yin, "The Effects of Medical Debt Relief: Evidence From Two Randomized Experiments," Working Paper 32315, National Bureau of Economic Research, April 2024. http://www.nber.org/papers/w32315.

Kowdley, Gopal, and Darwin Ashbaker. "Health Care Costs in America—Technology As a Major Driver." *Journal of Surgical Education* 68, no. 3 (May 1, 2011): 231–38. https://doi.org/10.1016/j.jsurg.2010.12.011.

Lakdawalla, Darius N. "Economics of the Pharmaceutical Industry." *Journal of Economic Literature* 56, no. 2 (2018): 397–449. https://doi.org/10.1257/jel.20161327.

Legerski, Elizabeth Miklya, and Justin Allen Berg. "Americans' Approval of the 2010 Affordable Care Act: Self-Interest and Symbolic Politics*." *Sociological Inquiry* 86, no. 3 (August 1, 2016): 285–300. https://doi.org/10.1111/soin.12121.

Light, Donald W. "Introduction: Ironies of Success: A New History of the American Health Care 'System.'" *Journal of Health and Social Behavior* 45 (2004): 1–24.

Long, Michael J, James D Chesney, Richard P Ament, Susan I DesHarnais, Steven T Fleming, Edward J Kobrinski, and Brenda S Marshall. "The Effect of PPS on Hospital Product and Productivity." *Medical Care*, 1987, 528–38.

Lopes, Lunna, Audrey Kearney, Alex Montero, Liz Hamel, and Mollyann Brodie. "Health Care Debt in the US: The Broad Consequences of Medical and Dental Bills." *Kaiser Family Foundation* 16 (2022).

Lopez, Eric, Tricia Neuman, Gretchen Jacobsen, and Larry Levitt. "How Much More Than Medicare Do Private Insurers Pay? A Review of the Literature." Kaiser Family Foundation, April 15, 2020. https://www.kff.org/medicare/issue-brief/how-much-more-than-medicare-do-private-insurers-pay-a-review-of-the-literature/.

Luhby, Tami. "These Are the First 10 Drugs Subject to Medicare Price Negotiations." *CNN*, August 29, 2023. https://www.cnn.com/2023/08/29/politics/medicare-drug-price-negotiations/index.html.

Lutz, Sandy, and Erin Preston Gee. *The For-Profit Healthcare Revolution: The Growing Impact of Investor-Owned Health Systems in America.* Probus Professional Publishing, 1995.

Marks, Jonathan H. "Lessons from Corporate Influence in the Opioid Epidemic: Toward a Norm of Separation." *Journal of Bioethical Inquiry* 17, no. 2 (2020): 173–89. https://doi.org/10.1007/s11673-020-09982-x.

Marlowe, Joseph, and Paul Sullivan. "Medical Tourism: The Ultimate Outsourcing." *Human Resource Planning*, June 2007. Gale Academic OneFile.

Martin, Edward D. "The Federal Initiative in Rural Health." *Public Health Reports (1974-)* 90, no. 4 (1975): 291–97.

Mayes, Rick, and Robert E. Hurley. "Pursuing Cost Containment in a Pluralistic Payer Environment: From the Aftermath of Clinton's Failure at Health Care Reform to the Balanced Budget Act of 1997." *Health Economics, Policy and Law* 1, no. 3 (2006): 237–61. https://doi.org/10.1017/S1744133106003033.

McArthur, John H., and Francis D. Moore. "The Two Cultures and the Health Care Revolution: Commerce and Professionalism in Medical Care." *JAMA* 277, no. 12 (March 26, 1997): 985–89. https://doi.org/10.1001/jama.1997.03540360053031.

McFarlane, Joshua, Jerry Riggins, and Thomas J Smith. "SPIKE $: A Six-Step Protocol for Delivering Bad News about the Cost of Medical Care." *Journal of Clinical Oncology* 26, no. 25 (2008): 4200–4204.

Mechanic, David. *The Growth of Bureaucratic Medicine: An Inquiry Into the Dynamics of Patient Behavior and the Organization of Medical Care.* London: Wiley, 1976.

MedPac. "March 2020 Report to the Congress: Medicare Payment Policy," March 13, 2020.

Melnick, Glenn, Emmett Keeler, and Jack Zwanziger. "Market Power And Hospital Pricing: Are Nonprofits Different? New Evidence Suggests That in a Consolidated Market, Market Share May Be What Drives Hospitals' Pricing Behavior." *Health Affairs* 18, no. 3 (1999): 167–73.

Moe, Terry M. "Political Institutions: The Neglected Side of the Story." *Journal of Law, Economics, & Organization* 6, no. special (1990): 213–53. https://doi.org/10.1093/jleo/6.special_issue.213.

Moyniham, Roy and Alan Cassels. *Selling Sickness: How the World's Biggest Pharmaceutical Companies Are Turning Us All Into Patients.* New York: Nation Books, 2005.

Montgomery, Kathryn. *How Doctors Think: Clinical Judgment and the Practice of Medicine.* Oxford: Oxford University Press, 2006.

Mulligan, Casey. "The Value of Pharmacy Benefit Management." Working Paper. NBER Working Paper Series. National Bureau of Economic Research, July 2022. http://www.nber.org/papers/w30231.

Murthy, Vasudeva N. R., and Natalya Ketenci. "Is Technology Still a Major Driver of Health Expenditure in the United States? Evidence from Cointegration Analysis with Multiple Structural Breaks." *International Journal of Health Economics and Management* 17, no. 1

(2017): 29–50.

National Opinion Research Center. "Americans' Views on Healthcare Costs, Coverage and Policy." Chicago: University of Chicago, 2018.

National Research Council. "Controlling the Supply of Hospital Beds: A Policy Statement." Washington, D.C.: National Academy of Sciences, 1976.

Newhouse, J P. "An Iconoclastic View of Health Cost Containment." *Health Affairs* 12 Suppl, no. suppl 1 (1993): 152–71. https://doi.org/10.1377/hlthaff.12.suppl_1.152.

Newhouse, Joseph P. "Medical Care Costs: How Much Welfare Loss?" *The Journal of Economic Perspectives* 6, no. 3 (1992): 3–21.

Numbers, Ronald L. *Almost Persuaded: American Physicians and Compulsory Health Insurance, 1912-1920*. Baltimore: Johns Hopkins University Press, 1978.

Nyman, John A. "The Economics of Moral Hazard Revisited." *Journal of Health Economics* 18, no. 6 (December 1, 1999): 811–24. https://doi.org/10.1016/S0167-6296(99)00015-6.

Oberlander, Jonathan. "Learning from Failure in Health Care Reform." *New England Journal of Medicine* 357, no. 17 (October 25, 2007): 1677–79. https://doi.org/10.1056/NEJMp078201.

———. "Long Time Coming: Why Health Reform Finally Passed." *Health Affairs* 29, no. 6 (2010): 1112–16. https://doi.org/10.1377/hlthaff.2010.0447.

O'Connor, Gerald T, Hebe B Quinton, Neal D Traven, Lawrence D Ramunno, T Andrew Dodds, Thomas A Marciniak, and John E Wennberg. "Geographic Variation in the Treatment of Acute Myocardial Infarction: The Cooperative Cardiovascular Project." *Jama* 281, no. 7 (1999): 627–33.

Osborn, Robin, David Squires, Michelle M. Doty, Dana O. Sarnak, and Eric C. Schneider. "In New Survey Of Eleven Countries, US Adults Still Struggle With Access To And Affordability Of Health Care." *Health Affairs* 35, no. 12 (2016): 2327–36. https://doi.org/10.1377/hlthaff.2016.1088.

Parente, Stephen T, Roger Feldman, Joanne Spetz, Bryan Dowd, and Emily Egan Baggett. "Wage Growth for the Health Care Workforce: Projecting the Affordable Care Act Impact." *Health Services Research* 52, no. 2 (2017): 741. https://doi.org/10.1111/1475-6773.12498.

Paul-Shaheen, Pamela, and Eugenia S. Carpenter. "Legislating Hospital Bed

Reduction: The Michigan Experience." *Journal of Health Politics, Policy and Law* 6, no. 4 (August 1, 1982): 653–75. https://doi.org/10.1215/03616878-6-4-653.

Pauly, Mark V. "The Economics of Moral Hazard: Comment." *The American Economic Review* 58, no. 3 (1968): 531–37.

Pauly, Mark V, and Peter Wilson. "Hospital Output Forecasts and the Cost of Empty Hospital Beds." *Health Services Research* 21, no. 3 (1986): 403.

Petersen, Melody. *Our Daily Meds : How the Pharmaceutical Companies Transformed Themselves into Slick Marketing Machines and Hooked the Nation on Prescription Drugs.* 1st ed. New York: Farrar, Straus and Giroux, 2008.

Phelps, Charles, and Cathleen Mooney. "Variations in Medical Practice Use: Causes and Consequences." In *Competitive Approaches to Health Care Reform.*, edited by Richard Arnould, Robert Rich, and William White. Washington, D.C.: Urban Institute Press, 1993. https://urresearch.rochester.edu/institutionalPublicationPublicView.action?institutionalItemVersionId=2402.

Pollitz, Karen, Jennifer Tolbert, and Rosa Ma. "Survey of Health Insurance Marketplace Assister Programs." *Kaiser Family Foundation* 15 (2014).

Porter, Dorothy. *Health, Civilization, and the State: A History of Public Health from Ancient to Modern Times.* London; Routledge, 1999.

Powell, J A, M Darvell, and J A M Gray. "The Doctor, The Patient and the World-Wide Web: How the Internet Is Changing Healthcare." *Journal of the Royal Society of Medicine* 96, no. 2 (February 1, 2003): 74–76. https://doi.org/10.1177/014107680309600206.

Quadagno, Jill. *One Nation, Uninsured: Why the U.S. Has No National Health Insurance* (Oxford: Oxford University Press, 2006)

Rajkumar, Vincent. "The High Cost of Prescription Drugs: Causes and Solutions." *Blood Cancer Journal (New York)* 10, no. 6 (2020): 71–71. https://doi.org/10.1038/s41408-020-0338-x.

Ransford, H Edward, PhD, Frank R Carrillo PhD, and Yessenia Rivera MD. "Health Care-Seeking among Latino Immigrants: Blocked Access, Use of Traditional Medicine, and the Role of Religion." *Journal of Health Care for the Poor and Underserved* 21, no. 3 (August 2010): 862–78. https://doi.org/10.1353/hpu.0.0348.

Raudenbush, Danielle T. *Health Care off the Books: Poverty, Illness, and Strategies for Survival in Urban America.* Oakland, California: University of California Press, 2020. https://doi. org/10.1525/9780520973602.

Rayack, Elton. *Professional Power and American Medicine: The Economics of the American Medical Association.* World Series in Economics. Cleveland: World Pub. Co., 1967c.

———. "The American Medical Association and the Development of Voluntary Insurance: Part I." *Social Policy & Administration* 1, no. 2 (1967a): 3–25. https://doi.org/10.1111/j.1467-9515.1967. tb00054.x.

———. "The American Medical Association and the Development of Voluntary Insurance: Part II." *Social Policy & Administration* 1, no. 3 (1967b): 29–55. https://doi.org/10.1111/j.1467-9515.1967. tb00063.x.

Relman, Arnold S. "Cost Control, Doctors' ethics, and Patient Care." *Issues in Science and Technology* 1, no. 2 (1985): 103–11.

———. "The New Medical-Industrial Complex." *New England Journal of Medicine* 303, no. 17 (1980): 963–70.

Reverby, S. "Stealing the Golden Eggs: Ernest Amory Codman and the Science and Management of Medicine." *Bulletin of the History of Medicine* 55, no. 2 (1981): 156–71.

Rice, Thomas H. "The Impact of Changing Medicare Reimbursement Rates on Physician-Induced Demand." *Medical Care* 21, no. 8 (1983): 803–15.

Richman, Ilana B., and Mollyann Brodie. "A National Study of Burdensome Health Care Costs among Non-Elderly Americans." *BMC Health Services Research* 14, no. 1 (2014): 435–435. https://doi. org/10.1186/1472-6963-14-435.

Robbins, Rebecca and Reed Abelson. "The Opaque Industry Secretly Inflating Prices for Prescription Drugs," *The New York Times* (June 21, 2024).

Robinson, James C. *The Corporate Practice of Medicine: Competition and Innovation in Health Care.* Berkeley: University of California Press, 1999.

Robinson, James C, and Harold S Luft. "Competition and the Cost of Hospital Care, 1972 to 1982." *JAMA : The Journal of the American Medical Association* 257, no. 23 (1987): 3241–45. https://doi. org/10.1001/jama.1987.03390230077028.

Rosenberg, Charles E. "Medical Text and Social Context: Explaining

William Buchan's 'Domestic Medicine'." *Bulletin of the History of Medicine* 57, no. 1 (1983): 22–42.

Rosenthal, Elisabeth. *An American Sickness: How Healthcare Became Big Business and How You Can Take it Back*. (New York: Penguin, 2018).

Rosenthal, Elisabeth. "A Peek at Big Pharma's Playbook That Leaves Many Americans Unable to Afford Their Drugs." *The Louisiana Weekly* 97, no. 51 (2023): 6.

Russell, Louise B. "Technology in Hospitals: Medical Advances and Their Diffusion." *Health Care Management Review* 4, no. 4 (1979): 86.

Scheffler, Richard M., Dolores G. Clement, Sean D. Sullivan, Teh-wei Hu, and Hai-Yen Sung. "The Hospital Response to Medicare's Prospective Payment System: An Econometric Model of Blue Cross and Blue Shield Plans." *Medical Care* 32, no. 5 (1994): 471–85.

Schoen, Cathy, and Sara R Collins. "The Big Five Health Insurers' Membership And Revenue Trends: Implications For Public Policy." *Health Affairs* 36, no. 12 (2017): 2185–94. https://doi.org/10.1377/hlthaff.2017.0858.

Schwartz, Jerome L. "Early History of Prepaid Medical Care Plans." *Bulletin of the History of Medicine* 39 (1965): 450.

Schwartz, Lisa M., and Steven Woloshin. "Medical Marketing in the United States, 1997-2016." *JAMA* 321, no. 1 (January 1, 2019): 80–96. https://doi.org/10.1001/jama.2018.19320.

Shrank, William H., Teresa L. Rogstad, and Natasha Parekh. "Waste in the US Health Care System: Estimated Costs and Potential for Savings." *JAMA* 322, no. 15 (October 15, 2019): 1501–9. https://doi.org/10.1001/jama.2019.13978.

Simborg, Donald W. "DRG Creep: A New Hospital-Acquired Disease." *New England Journal of Medicine* 304, no. 26 (1981): 1602–4.

"Single-Payer Health Care Systems: Issues and Options." Washington, D.C.: U.S. Government Printing Office, 1994.

Skocpol, Theda. *Boomerang: Health Care Reform and the Turn Against Government*. New York: Norton, 1996.

Sloan, Frank A., Michael A. Morrisey, and Joseph Valvona. "Effects of the Medicare Prospective Payment System on Hospital Cost Containment: An Early Appraisal." *The Milbank Quarterly* 66, no. 2 (1988): 191–220. https://doi.org/10.2307/3350030.

Stabile, Mark, and Sarah Thomson. "The Changing Role of Government in Financing Health Care: An International Perspective." *Journal of Economic Literature* 52, no. 2 (2014): 480–518. https://doi.org/10.1257/jel.52.2.480.

Starr, Paul. *The Social Transformation of American Medicine: The Rise of a Sovereign Profession and the Making of a Vast Industry*. Hachette UK, 2017.

Steinberg, Richard, and Bradford H Gray. "' The Role of Nonprofit Enterprise' in 1993: Hansmann Revisited." *Nonprofit and Voluntary Sector Quarterly* 22, no. 4 (1993): 297–316.

Stevens, Rosemary. *In Sickness and In Wealth: American Hospitals in the Twentieth Century*. New York: Basic Books, 1989.

Stewart, Kenneth. "The Experimental Consumer Price Index for Elderly Americans (CPI-E): 1982-2007." *Monthly Labor Review* 131, no. April (2008): 19.

Stoline, Anne, and Jonathan P Weiner. "The New Medical Marketplace: A Physician's Guide to the Health Care Revolution," 1988.

Stone, G. A., Fernandez, M., & DeSantiago, A. "Rural Latino health and the built environment: a systematic review," *Ethnicity & Health*, 27:1 (2019), 1–26. https://doi.org/10.1080/13557858.2019.1606899.

Stowe, Steven M. "Seeing Themselves at Work: Physicians and the Case Narrative in the Mid-Nineteenth-Century American South." *The American Historical Review* 101, no. 1 (1996): 41–79. https://doi.org/10.1086/ahr/101.1.41.

Straube, Barry. "A Role for Government: An Observation on Federal Healthcare Efforts in Prevention." *American Journal of Preventive Medicine* 44, no. 1 (2013): S39-42. https://doi.org/10.1016/j.amepre.2012.09.009.

Stump, Tammy K., Naa Eghan, Brian L. Egleston, Olivia Hamilton, Melanie Pirollo, J. Sanford Schwartz, Katrina Armstrong, J. Robert Beck, Neal J. Meropol, and Yu-Ning Wong. "Cost Concerns of Patients With Cancer." *Journal of Oncology Practice* 9, no. 5 (September 1, 2013): 251–57. https://doi.org/10.1200/JOP.2013.000929.

Thomasson, Melissa A. "From Sickness to Health: The Twentieth-Century Development of U.S. Health Insurance." *Explorations in Economic History* 39, no. 3 (July 1, 2002): 233–53. https://doi.org/10.1006/exeh.2002.0788.

Thomasson, Melissa A. "The Importance of Group Coverage: How Tax Policy Shaped U.S. Health Insurance." *The American Economic Review* 93, no. 4 (2003): 1373–84. https://doi.org/10.1257/000282803769206359.

Thorpe, Kenneth E, Curtis S Florence, David H Howard, and Peter Joski. "The Rising Prevalence of Treated Disease: Effects on Private Health Insurance Spending." *Health Affairs (Millwood, Va.)* Suppl Web Exclusives (2005): W5-317-W5-325.

Tilburt, Jon C, Matthew K Wynia, Robert D Sheeler, Bjorg Thorsteinsdottir, Katherine M James, Jason S Egginton, Mark Liebow, Samia Hurst, Marion Danis, and Susan Dorr Goold. "Views of US Physicians about Controlling Health Care Costs." *Jama* 310, no. 4 (2013): 380–89.

Tomes, Nancy. "Merchants of Health: Medicine and Consumer Culture in the United States, 1900–1940." *The Journal of American History (Bloomington, Ind.)* 88, no. 2 (2001): 519–47. https://doi.org/10.2307/2675104.

Tomes, Nancy. *Remaking the American Patient: How Madison Avenue and Modern Medicine Turned Patients Into Consumers*. Chapel Hill: University of North Carolina Press, 2016.

Tulum, Öner, and William Lazonick. "Financialized Corporations in a National Innovation System: The U.S. Pharmaceutical Industry." *International Journal of Political Economy* 47, no. 3–4 (2018): 281–316. https://doi.org/10.1080/08911916.2018.1549842.

VanderHei, Jim, Mike Allen, and Roy Schwartz. *Smart Brevity: The Power of Saying More With Less*. New York: Workman Publishing Company, 2022.

Viswanathan, Madhu, Raj Echambadi, Srinivas Venugopal, and Srinivas Sridharan. "Subsistence Entrepreneurship, Value Creation, and Community Exchange Systems: A Social Capital Explanation." *Journal of Macromarketing* 34, no. 2 (June 1, 2014): 213–26. https://doi.org/10.1177/0276146714521635.

Wagner, Lynn. "Healthcare Reform Lobbyists Assail Some of Panel's Stringent Cost Containment Ideas." *Modern Healthcare*, March 2, 1992.

Ward, Patricia Spain. "United States versus American Medical Association et al.: The Medical Antitrust Case of 1938-1943." *American Studies* 30, no. 2 (1989): 123–53.

Weisz, George, Alberto Cambrosio, Peter Keating, Loes Knaapen, Thomas Schlich, and Virginie J Tournay. "The Emergence of Clinical Practice Guidelines." *The Milbank Quarterly* 85, no. 4 (2007): 691–727. https://doi.org/10.1111/j.1468-0009.2007.00505.x.

Wennberg, J E. "Dealing with Medical Practice Variations: A Proposal for Action." *Health Affairs (Millwood, Va.)* 3, no. 2 (1984): 6–33. https://doi.org/10.1377/hlthaff.3.2.6.

Wennberg, John, and Alan Gittelsohn. "Variations in Medical Care among Small Areas." *Scientific American* 246, no. 4 (1982): 120–35.

Wilson, Fernando A., Leah Zallman, José A. Pagán. "Comparison of Use of Health Care Services and Spending for Unauthorized Immigrants vs Authorized Immigrants or US Citizens Using a Machine Learning Model," *JAMA Network Open* 3:12 (2020), doi:10.1001/jamanetworkopen.2020.29230.

Winant, Gabriel. *The next Shift: The Fall of Industry and the Rise of Health Care in Rust Belt America.* Harvard University Press, 2021.

Woolhandler, Steffie, and David U. Himmelstein. "Costs of Care and Administration at For-Profit and Other Hospitals in the United States." *New England Journal of Medicine* 336, no. 11 (March 13, 1997): 769–74. https://doi.org/10.1056/NEJM199703133361106.

Woolhandler, Steffie, and David U Himmelstein. "Extreme Risk—the New Corporate Proposition for Physicians." *New England Journal of Medicine* 333, no. 25 (1995): 1706–8.

Wouters, Olivier J, Martin McKee, and Jeroen Luyten. "Estimated Research and Development Investment Needed to Bring a New Medicine to Market, 2009-2018." *JAMA : The Journal of the American Medical Association* 323, no. 9 (2020): 844–53. https://doi.org/10.1001/jama.2020.1166.

Yin, Nina. "Pharmaceuticals, Incremental Innovation and Market Exclusivity." *International Journal of Industrial Organization* 87 (2023): 102922. https://doi.org/10.1016/j.ijindorg.2023.102922.

Yin, Wesley. "Market Incentives and Pharmaceutical Innovation." *Journal of Health Economics* 27, no. 4 (July 1, 2008): 1060–77. https://doi.org/10.1016/j.jhealeco.2008.01.002.

www.ingramcontent.com/pod-product-compliance
Lightning Source LLC
Chambersburg PA
CBHW070248290326
41930CB00042B/2858